s America

With a new preface by the authors

JOHN A. HALL AND CHARLES LINDHOLM

Is America breaking apart?

PRINCETON

UNIVERSITY

PRESS

PRINCETON

AND OXFORD

Copyright © 1999 by Princeton University Press

Published by Princeton University Press, 41 William Street, Princeton, New Jersey 08540

In the United Kingdom: Princeton University Press, 3 Market Place, Woodstock, Oxfordshire OX20 1SY

Third printing, and first paperback printing, with a new preface, 2001
Paperback ISBN 0-691-09011-4

The Library of Congress has cataloged the cloth edition of this book as follows

Hall, John A., 1949–

    Is America breaking apart? / John A. Hall and Charles Lindholm.

      p.   cm.

    Includes bibliographical references and index.

    ISBN 0-691-00410-2 (cl : alk. paper)

    1. United States — Social conditions — 1980–   2. Social values — United States.   3. National characteristics, American. 4. Sociology — United States.   5. United States — Politics and government — Philosophy.   I. Lindholm, Charles, 1946– II. Title.

    HN59.2.H34   1999   98-27793

    306′ .0973 — dc21

British Library Cataloging-in-Publication Data is available

This book has been composed in Electra

The lyric on page vii is reprinted by permission. Copyright © 1993 Sony/ ATV Songs LLC. All rights administered by Sony/ATV Music Publishing, 8 Music Square West, Nashville, TN 37023. All rights reserved.

Printed on acid-free paper. ∞

www.pup.princeton.edu

Printed in the United States of America

10 9 8 7 6 5 4 3

TO LINDA, MOLLY, AND CHERRY

Democracy is coming to the U.S.A.

It's coming to America first,

The cradle of the best and the worst.

It's here they got the range

And the machinery for change

And it's here they got the spiritual thirst . . .

Democracy is coming to the U.S.A.

LEONARD COHEN

"Democracy"

Contents

Preface to the Paperback Edition

One of the joys of intellectual life lies in its essential unpredictability, with the best-laid plans for the success of a book often proving to be illusory. So we are very gratified that our simple observations about the continued stability and power of the United States seemed to strike a general chord, placing us in a position to write this preface to a paperback edition. This is not to say that our arguments have completely swept the field! Very much to the contrary, the seemingly endless complaints about the tearing of the social fabric of the United States and the decline of its culture have continued unabated — perhaps, indeed, have become even more heated.

This can be seen at the purely intellectual level by the media attention paid to varied laments decrying the erosion of American society. The title of a recent book by Gertrude Himmelfarb, *One Nation: Two Cultures*,[1] nicely encapsulates the tenor of this genre. The book draws a contrast between liberal, hedonistic, secular postmodernists, located in urban and industrial areas and on the coasts, and conservative, moralistic, traditionally religious, family-value advocates, generally resident in the rural heartland of the South and the West. This conflict in values between these two purportedly incommensurable social worlds has led, it is claimed, to a schizophrenic America, bereft of a coherent civil society and impotent to act against pervasive ethical relativism and moral decline.

This scenario of shattering division gained rather general credence as a result of the remarkable presidential race of 2000. Many commentators proclaimed that two cultures were in evidence. George W. Bush, the hero of the conservative and the righteous, swept the South and West, while Al Gore, an earnest liberal, won on both coasts and in the industrial Midwest, leaving the election to be decided in the virtually evenly

---

[1] G. Himmelfarb, *One Nation: Two Cultures* (New York: Alfred Knopf, 1999).

divided state of Florida. In the turmoil of the ensuing weeks various officials and courts ruled on the validity of dimpled chads, while irate partisans of the two candidates exchanged accusations and invective. Writing in the *Washington Post* just after the election, the dean of American political commentators, David Broder, warned darkly that the nation had rarely appeared to be more divided.[2] His colleague Richard Cohen even repudiated Gore, for whom he had voted, so as to reluctantly embrace Bush simply because he thought Bush could better act as a conciliator to heal the terrible rift threatening to destroy the country.[3]

In a manner that seemed to justify these fears, many Democratic activists angrily questioned the integrity of the American legal system when the conservative majority of the Supreme Court finally handed the presidency to Bush. In so doing, they had, as Vincent Bugliosi fulminated, "gotten away with murder."[4] Reflecting this heated atmosphere, British columnist Hugo Young claimed that "the United States presidential election has been a calamity without precedent. Its result will not be accepted by large numbers of Americans. . . . Democracy, quite simply, was poisoned to put George W. Bush in the White House."[5] Meanwhile, Bush's advocates, exulting in victory, taunted the sore losers of the Left. The appearance of acrimonious opposing camps, unlikely ever to be reconciled, seemed to be supported by statistical evidence. In a typical example, a poll in mid-December found that 49 percent of

[2] D. Broder cited in M. Kettle, "A House Divided Has Shaky Foundations," *Guardian Weekly*, November 16–22, 2000, 6.

[3] R. Cohen, "I Voted for Gore, Now I'm Not So Sure That He's the Man to Do the Job," reprinted in *Guardian Weekly*, November 30–December 6, 2000, 27.

[4] V. Bugliosi, "None Dare Call It Treason," *The Nation*, February 5, 2001, 19.

[5] H. Young, "Democracy Was Poisoned to Give Bush the White House," *Guardian Weekly*, December 21–27, 2000, 10.

respondents wanted Gore to withdraw and 47 percent wanted the exact opposite.[6] This division reflected the actual electoral results, which were amazingly close, and seemed to reveal a society desperately at odds with itself.

But all of this *Sturm und Drang* has not made us change our views. To the contrary, the flood of complaint and the hand-wringing anxiety of moralistic pundits and columnists about the dire fate of America reinforces one of our initial points — that Americans like to be scared about the fragility of their society, despite its obvious stability and power. Any book that preys on this propensity is bound to sell — which is the reason we did not entitle our book *Why America Isn't Breaking Apart*! We argue at length within that the unrealistic fear Americans feel about the collapse and disintegration of their society is due to their historically derived faith that their nation is destined to lead the world to salvation — or to be damned in the attempt. Furthermore, the individualistic and anti-state culture of the United States makes it very difficult for citizens to recognize communal and structural sources of strength. From within this worldview, any internal conflict is likely to be seen as potentially ruinous, and is the focus of immoderate attention and anxiety.

But leaving aside the general propensity of Americans to fret obsessively about the supposed frailty of the nation, our general views can be underlined by commenting on two issues mentioned. Let us begin with the nature of culture, and then turn to our own, rather different assessment of the election.

Himmelfarb's book, and the commentary it inspired, suffers from a basic and very American misapprehension about the real nature of culture. The assumption is that culture is a unitary, wholly integrated, and quite conscious system of values in

---

[6] Cited in M. Kettle, "Republicans Look to Divide and Rule," *Guardian Weekly*, December 14–20, 2000, 6.

which people agree more or less about everything. No culture at any time can meet this exacting requirement. Instead, culture can best be defined as a shared way of approaching reality that is simply taken for granted, largely outside the realm of consciousness. It is just "the way things are." The United States does have such a shared perspective, based largely on a deep faith in the autonomy, equality, and freedom of each individual to choose his or her own destiny. The exact nature of the internal contradictions, tensions, and permutations of this culturally specific worldview need not unduly concern us here for they are a major topic of the pages that follow. But it is worth insisting that the presence of such oppositions in the United States is "normal"—for oppositions exist within every extant cultural context. Americans can and do disagree about key issues—how freedom can best be realized and how equality is to be reconciled with autonomy—but they do so in good faith, and without becoming irreconcilably divided into "two cultures." In fact, we suggest that internal arguments within the United States are premised to a truly remarkable extent on common assumptions about basic principles.

Nor is conflict within a cultural framework a catastrophe. It only becomes so when disagreement is envisioned, as it is in Himmelfarb's book, as total and exclusive, without the possibility of common ground between the opposing sides. That would indeed be the way to relativism, perhaps even to solipsism. But a normal culture is altogether different, the provider of a common language in which disagreement can be couched so that argument occurs at points where internal contradictions exist. Discussion, conflict, and even antagonism are signs of the strength and adaptability of a culture, not of weakness, which is signaled by rigidity, demonization, and repression. It is precisely because Americans share a culture that they can be so flexible, adaptive, and tolerant of one another. It is this commonality that obliges Himmelfarb to conclude, despite herself, that the "two cultures" are not in fact at war at all, but actually live together "without civil strife or anarchy."[7]

Next, let us turn to the election. There are several points to make here. For one thing, what in fact were the great issues that threatened to tear the social fabric apart? The size of a tax cut? In actuality, what was most noticeable was the extraordinarily narrow range of public "difference" between the two candidates, which contributed greatly to the high degree of disinterest shown by the American electorate prior to the vote. Nor do the election results really demonstrate any fundamental division between North and South, liberal and conservative, rural and urban, or religious and secular. As ever, a closer look reveals instead a much more complex picture — one in which Gore and Bush actually shared votes in almost every state. Clearly, traditional blocs, such as Blacks and Latinos, are becoming far more politically mixed due to social mobility and demographic shifts. And, while broad traditional divisions of city and country, Bible Belt and Rust Belt remained relevant in the overall vote, it is also worth recalling that the country has become ever more suburban in makeup (50 percent) and ever more upper middle class (40 percent). These people make up the majority of Americans who declare themselves political moderates, and who strongly dislike partisan politics. They cast their votes for Bush and Gore primarily for pragmatic reasons, not because of deeply felt ideological appeal by either candidate.[8] Indeed, this is the case for most American voters, who are repelled by zealotry and prefer a leader who is bland and comforting. Accordingly, Bush's folksy campaign stressed that he trusted the people (not the government), and was one of them, friendly and easygoing — the kind of guy with whom you

---

[7] Himmelfarb, *One Nation: Two Cultures*, 146.

[8] Data drawn from "Bush's America: One Nation, Fairly Divisible, under God," *The Economist*, January 20, 2000, 21–23.

could have a beer. Divisive moral issues such as abortion were played down in his campaign, which equally went to great lengths to minimize the influence of the Religious Right. In contrast, Gore's serious, hectoring personality and his connection to "big government" cost him votes, as did his principled distancing from Clinton, who remained the most popular president in modern times despite (or perhaps because of) those all-too-human moral flaws that made him "just like us."

But the major point is that the behavior of the electorate during the process verified, as nothing else could, our point about the stability of the American system. Consider the situation. The charge at the time was of a stolen election. The historical norm in such situations is severe conflict — at a minimum massive street protests, at a maximum genuine social revolution. Exactly this happened in the case of Yugoslavia, leading to the downfall of Slobodan Milosevic. The anger felt by Democratic political activists at dubious legal decisions of the Supreme Court — exacerbated by the fact that Bush's father had been both head of the CIA and president, while his brother was the Florida governor whose campaign manager was in charge of vote counting — suggested a real potential for resistance against the injustice of the final result. Nothing of the sort occurred. Instead, only a short time after the United States Supreme Court proclaimed an end to the recounts (a decision opposed by 60 percent of the public) polls showed that 80 percent were glad Bush was president.[9] Further, despite dire predictions, there have been no popular uprisings against Bush and his administration, nor has political life itself been notably more acrimonious. It seems evident that most Americans, after having been stimulated to an abnormal state of partisanship by the excitement of a close contest, have now re-

[9] Cited in M. Kettle, "Will History Be Kind to Bill?" *Guardian Weekly*, December 28, 2000–January 3, 2001, 2.

turned to their normal state of bored disinterest in politics — a boredom, it should be recalled, that was widespread prior to the election itself, which was remarkable primarily for the colorlessness of the two candidates. These facts should teach us that political commentators in the United States are quite wrong to mistake their own passions for the passions of the American people. As Martin Kettle wisely noted soon after the election, "As long as the sun comes up in the morning, there's food in the fridge, something to watch on the television and ordinary life is tolerably possible, politicians are going to be somewhere in the back of people's minds, not near the front of them."[10] Only if the economy goes very sour will Americans again wake up and exercise their political muscle by "voting the bum out."

We can end this preface by reiterating that our intent in writing this book was primarily descriptive. We wanted to show our readers, as objectively as possible, what the United States looks like from a cultural anthropological and socio-historical perspective, and to thereby reveal some of the reasons it has achieved its extraordinary power and its authority on the world stage. We did not wish to pass judgments, either positive or negative, on what we found. But while remaining value-neutral, we also wanted to reveal some of the internal tensions in the society, and dissect the taken-for-granted values that motivate it. We especially hoped to show the way in which American values mask or deny deep inequities, particularly those of race and class. Our picture of the United States is therefore not one of a perfect society. Indeed, the United States is in many ways very imperfect, and all the more so for refusing to recognize its real problems. But, whether we like it or not, it is an amazingly strong and secure society, and will remain so for the foreseeable future.

[10] Ibid.

Preface

This book is the result of a discovery made in the midst of conversation about the sudden academic interest in identity politics. We came to realize that we shared a perception, best expressed in the form of an injunction: forget the endless talk of difference, note that everyone is saying the same thing! In other words, the fact that anxiety about culture war is *shared* is itself evidence of the continuing homogeneity of American life.

Our skepticism about the supposedly broken state of the union reflects our backgrounds. As an American anthropologist who has worked on the Middle East and done research on charismatic social movements and a British comparative historical sociologist familiar with Northern Ireland and the post-communist world, we are all too familiar with societies genuinely torn by violent disorders. The United States is not such a society.[1] However, we seek to go beyond skepticism to offer an account of the manner in which America has come to be held together, and to weigh the positive and negative aspects of that unity.

Stephen Graubard suggested an article on this topic;[2] Peter Dougherty urged us to turn it into a book. We have benefited from the advice of Alan Wolfe, Mort Weinfeld, Anatoly Khazanov, Bob Wuthnow, Steve Kalberg, Rogers Brubaker, Cherry Lindholm, and Suzanne Staggenborg. We are indebted to all these friends, whether they share our views or not. It is worth noting, finally, that the writing of this book has been an enjoyable and wholly collaborative effort: we share responsibility for its contents.

---

[1] We usually refer to the United States as America. This is in part in deference to ordinary usage, and in part because "United Statesian" is not an accepted adjective.

[2] C. Lindholm and J. A. Hall, "Is America Falling Apart?" *Daedalus* 126 (1997): 183–210. Please note that our views have matured over the last year.

IS AMERICA BREAKING APART?

Introduction

Americans have long been fascinated with themselves in a way that Europeans have not. It is hard, for example, to imagine an Italian writing a book about "Italian exceptionalism," whereas such books are a staple of American social thought. Of course, it is perfectly obvious that all countries are equally "exceptional" in the simple sense that each has passed through a singular history and exhibits a unique social configuration. But Americans are exceptional in their concern with their own exceptionalism.

Americans believe themselves to have a special mission in the world. Their passion for self-interrogation is therefore not simply an expression of intellectual curiosity; instead, interrogation is usually also a form of self-laceration, a way to scourge American society for its inability to live up to its moral promise. Such high ethical ambitions and the accompanying anxiety about falling from grace date back to 1630, when John Winthrop, the first leader of the Massachusetts Bay Colony, called upon his congregation to join together in a covenant with God to build a "Citty upon a Hill." Winthrop warned his parishioners that should the community break the sacred covenant and "fall to embrace this present world and prosecute our carnall intencions seekeing great things for ourselves and our posterity, the Lord will surely breake out in wrathe against us."[1] Ever since, the fear of being forsaken, of losing purpose, of selfishly abandoning community and sinking into evil, has given a highly eschatological tone to the study of American history and society.

However, this tone has become especially shrill of late, as a

[1] Quoted in R. Bellah, *The Broken Covenant: American Civil Religion in Time of Trial*, 2d ed. (Chicago: University of Chicago Press, 1992), 14–15. For commentary on Winthrop's notion of the covenant, see P. Miller, *Errand into the Wilderness* (Cambridge: Harvard University Press, 1956), 148–49.

host of bestsellers has appeared claiming that the social fabric of the United States is unraveling.[2] Most assert that Americans have become so individualistic that they can no longer even conceptualize that a collectivity is required to create a compelling moral identity for its members. Robert Bellah and his associates make this point in *Habits of the Heart*; a variant upon this theme has been put forward with great force by Robert Putnam.[3] It seems that we are lonely, selfish, and unhappy. Equally somber voices suggest that Americans have become caged by group identities, not just of traditional ethnicities but of new groups, such as the Nation of Islam and the Queer Nation. From this perception derive the panicked outcries that America is in danger of being torn asunder by violent "culture wars."[4]

Clearly, there is a paradox here: Americans are imagined both to be conformists, unable to resist the tyranny of groups, and to be isolated amoral individualists! It seems that all sides agree on very little, save that the nation is confronted with terrible wrenching problems that threaten to shatter it completely. The intent of this book is to bring back to general attention the cohesive power of the American experiment. In it we will reveal the historically constructed institutional patterns

---

[2] The two most eloquent are A. Schlesinger, *The Disuniting of America: Reflections on a Multicultural Society* (Knoxville, Tenn.: Whittle Direct Books, 1992), and R. Hughes, *The Culture of Complaint: The Fraying of America* (New York: Warner Books, 1993).

[3] R. Bellah et al., *Habits of the Heart* (New York: Harper and Row, 1986); R. Putnam, "Bowling Alone," *Journal of Democracy* 6 (1995): 65–78, and "The Strange Disappearance of Civic America," *American Prospect* 24 (1996): 34–48.

[4] The most apocalyptic is J. D. Hunter in *Culture Wars: The Struggle to Define America* (New York: Basic Books, 1991) and *Before the Shooting Begins: Searching for Democracy in America's Culture War* (New York: Free Press, 1994).

and the shared cultural values of American society, all the while asking whether these institutional structures and cultural commonalities are enough to hold America together. To anticipate, our answer will be that, despite deep inner tensions, America is highly unlikely to suffer from the fragmentation and collapse so widely predicted by recent commentators.

To help turn readers toward our position, two preliminary points can usefully be made. First, social theorists are no better, and perhaps much worse, than normal citizens in their ability to distinguish ordinary conflict from destructive warfare. This inability is especially marked in America, where the demand for absolute harmony has deep ideological and historical roots. Under these circumstances, all dispute, however innocuous, can easily be considered ruinous. But this ignores the elementary fact that conflict can help create consensus.[5] In this, societies are much like marriages. Negotiation, discussion, and argument are forms of conflict, but they are also signs of life. In contrast, relationships that insist on complete harmony either know the peace of the dead or collapse in the divorce courts. Differently put, the recognition and regulation of conflict, as in the American constitutional system based on the alternation of parties, avoids the tectonic shifts of revolution and civil war. But conflict can intensify so as to lead to disaster, the more that different struggles become layered on top of one another.[6] In modern France, for example, to be on the political left necessarily meant that one was also secular: this was made inevitable because the old regime was underwritten by an official religion. Much of our discussion will explore how America

---

[5] G. Simmel, *Conflict and The Web of Group-Affiliations* (reprint, Glencoe, Ill.: Free Press, 1955). Cf. L. Coser, *The Functions of Social Conflict* (Glencoe, Ill.: Free Press, 1956).

[6] R. Dahrendorf, *Class and Class Conflict in Industrial Society*, rev. ed. (Stanford: Stanford University Press, 1959).

has successfully managed to avoid such divisive layering of region, class, religion, ethnicity, and race.

A second point concerns the way in which contemporary critical discourse assumes the individual and society to be polar opposites. In making this assumption critics follow Alexis de Tocqueville, the first and still the greatest analyst of America. A French nobleman who came to the United States in 1831, Tocqueville was a member of a postrevolutionary generation that was suspicious of democracy on the ground that the entry of the masses had led to the Terror. Much of what Tocqueville saw in America — conformity, an absence of standards, shallow materialism, a potential tyranny of the majority — did not excite his admiration. In particular, Tocqueville was deeply worried by the distinct possibility that apolitical American individuals would be so concerned with their self-interest as to withdraw from their political duties:

> I see an innumerable multitude of men, alike and equal, constantly circling around in pursuit of the petty and banal pleasures with which they glut their souls. Each one of them, withdrawn into himself, is almost unaware of the fate of the rest. Mankind, for him, consists in his children and his personal friends. As for the rest of his fellow citizens, they are near enough, but he does not notice them. He touches them but feels nothing.[7]

For Tocqueville, isolated American individuals are empty of everything save the desire to seek status and luxury, and will be prone to acquiesce passively in the tyranny of majority opinion and the despotism of the state. In order to resist this temptation, Tocqueville argued, the atomistic actor must somehow be given a sense of communal purpose: an active associational life

---

[7] A. de Tocqueville, *Democracy in America* (reprint, New York: Anchor Books, 1969), 691–92.

might at once function as insulation against the tyranny of the majority while also training people to take part as citizens in the larger life of the republic.

Tocqueville's low opinion of the isolated individual, and his related fear of the tyranny of the majority, are at the root of contemporary worries about both excessive autonomy and excessive conformity. While many of Tocqueville's insights are brilliant, on these central points we wish to take issue with him, preferring instead to follow the perspective offered by Max Weber.[8] The great German sociologist also came to the United States, although his 1904 visit is less celebrated.

While Tocqueville saw Americans as a formless heap of detached individuals who could gain moral resources only through group participation, Weber took a more positive approach:

> Whoever represents "democracy" as a mass fragmented into atoms, as our Romantics prefer to do, is fundamentally mistaken so far as the American democracy is concerned. "Atomization" is usually a consequence . . . of bureaucratic rationalism. . . . The genuine American society . . . was never such a sand pile.[9]

According to Weber what Tocqueville missed was the "sect spirit" of America, a spirit that is the legacy of its Protestant origins. This ethic links radical individualism with principled and self-aware voluntary participation in the larger moral com-

---

[8] M. Weber, "'Churches' and 'Sects' in North America," *Sociological Theory* 3 (1985): 7–11. Discussions of Weber's ideas about America are offered by S. Kim, "Of 'Sect Man': the Modern Self and Civil Society in Max Weber's Political Thought" (Ph.D. diss., University of Chicago, 1997), and S. Kalberg, "Tocqueville and Weber on the Sociological Origins of Citizenship: the Political Culture of American Democracy," *Citizenship Studies* 1 (1997): 199–222.

[9] Weber, "'Churches' and 'Sects' in North America," 10.

munity. Individualism and communal action are thereby united:

> [Sociability] in no way means a lessening of the individual's need to constantly attend to his self-affirmation. On the contrary, the task of *"proving" himself* is present more than ever *within* the group, in the circle of his associates. And thus, the social association to which the individual belongs is for him never something "organic," never a mystical total essence which floats over him and envelops him. Rather he is *always* completely conscious of it as a mechanism for his own material and ideal *ends*.[10]

Weber goes on to argue that American individuals are motivated by an internalized ethic of individual responsibility, personal honor, and principled resistance to immoral authority; they seek membership and participation in the community as a central measure of their own unique worth. This Protestant legacy means that instead of requiring groups to give them any sense of power and moral shape, American individuals already have a strong personal sense of their obligations and responsibilities, and voluntarily join (and leave) various communities in order to express and enact their own values. For Weber, the expansion of the sectarian spirit into ordinary life lends American society its extraordinary resilience. Explication of how this occurs will be another of our major themes.

Having established that conflict is not equivalent to collapse and individualism not necessarily without moral content, we can now characterize the argument to be made. First, the insistence that America is relatively stable should not be taken as triumphalism or as complacency. We are not in contact with Newt Gingrich, let alone in his pay. Crucially, we do not presume "order" to be always desirable; nor do we forget that re-

[10]Ibid., 11.

pression and injustice are very often involved in the creation and maintenance of stability. Our claim about American society should be seen in purely descriptive terms: we want to tell it like it is. If America is indeed, as Leonard Cohen sings, "the cradle of the best and the worst," then we are encouraged to have hopes for an extension of democracy to those groups presently marginalized, and especially to African Americans.[11] At the same time we remain uncertain whether such an extension will actually occur.

Second, we proceed by making broad use of the distinction drawn by British social anthropology between structure and culture. This division is imperfect. For one thing, it tends to ignore the forces of history. For another, it is evident that the line between structure and culture cannot be easily drawn: an education system seeks to instill cultural values but is equally properly seen as a key social institution, while racial prejudice is not just an attitude but also a question of the distribution of power. Nonetheless, the distinction will prove useful here as a heuristic device, especially since historical perspective is offered. It should be further noted that we have a high opinion of classic ethnographies of American life, and hope to bring them to their rightful place at the center of current debates.

In the first part of the book, we will show how American society has developed over time, how it has overcome divisions, and how its institutional structure has been formed. The specification of the precise ways in which the United States originated and in which it develops is slightly at odds with

---

[11] Some authors, notably Orlando Patterson, in *The Ordeal of Integration: Progress and Resentment in America's "Racial" Crisis* (Washington, D.C.: Counterpoint, 1997), have argued that the term African American should be reserved for recent immigrants from Africa, while long-term black residents of the the United States should be designated as Afro-Americans. While recognizing the usefulness of this distinction, we have chosen here to follow the more conventional terminology.

dominant interpretations: in particular, we stress moments of crisis and the suppression of alternative possibilities. The second part of the book focuses on the enduring ideals of American culture and the manner in which these ideals presently operate to buttress the existing social order. Simultaneously, we also record tensions within this cultural code, and especially concern ourselves with the invidious aspects of structure that the cultural lens distorts, obscures and denies. The conclusion considers the future of a society that imagines itself to be made up of diverse and autonomous individuals, while ignoring fundamental realities of hierarchy and class distinction; a society that asserts the equality of all, and still is stained by racism; a society that is in fact the most powerful and stable in the world, yet is perennially shaken by self-doubt and moral anguish.

The growth of political stability

PART ONE

REGRETTABLY, scholars who investigate social and political processes do not possess a neat set of neutral and uncontested terms. What is beneficial for some people may be catastrophic for others, with the balance between the two almost always hard to calibrate. Behind our relatively simple and straightforward account of the growth of political stability in the United States lurk many moral ambiguities. We intend to accentuate, rather than to hide from, such troubling areas of ambivalence and opposition.

However, this does not mean that we propose to mount a soapbox. Stability is taken in a strictly social 'scientific sense, that is, as the relatively unquestioned hegemony of a set of social arrangements — by which is meant the destruction or absence of genuine societal alternatives and the diminution of collective efforts, violent or otherwise, to achieve them. Stability may be — indeed, should be — judged from differing perspectives: the "peace" of the cold war felt very different in Prague than in London, just as the contemporary consensus in Washington between Speaker Gingrich and President Clinton looks altogether different to denizens of inner-city ghettos than it does to corporate executives. Our intent is to lay bare mechanisms of stability that will be recognized as such both by those who endorse and by those who contest the status quo.

Our argument analyzes the pattern of America's past. Our purpose is *not* to provide a skeletal narrative history, but rather to trace the gradual forging of a powerful national political structure. Four historical turning points are seen as crucial. Accounting for the creation of a popular national entity must be the initial task. How did a set of of disparate colonies manage to achieve union? Second, it is equally important to remember that unity then had to be maintained. America did nearly break apart as the result of slavery; only massive violence preserved the Union and emancipated the slaves, although racism continued to plague American society. The third historical moment is the challenge posed by white workers who rebelled against the confines of the industrial wage contract. The societal alternative that they proposed came to naught, with violence again playing a major role in its destruction. Finally, we argue that involvement with the wider world — especially military involvement — has done most to affect American political stability in the twentieth century. Two points stand out here. In the first place, military participation together with the desire to lead by example helped to occasion domestic reform, especially in the area of civil rights. In the second place, the hegemonic power of the United States within the world political economy means that its internal social arrangements are not likely to change as the result of external pressures.

The state and the people

The establishment of a stable federal government in America was not a foregone conclusion. In fact, a mood of considerable pessimism reigned among the revolutionary leaders in the years immediately following independence. Virtue seemed to have deserted the new republic, putting its continued existence into doubt. One problem was that of containing popular revolutionary enthusiasm. Rebellions like that of Daniel Shay suggested that the country was becoming ungovernable, with the privileged class position of the elite accordingly being put at risk. Much radical agitation took place at the state level, thereby highlighting a second problem. For the newly independent colonies, national unity was a matter of acute concern. The confluence of different local cultures and interests within America meant that loyalty to states, regions, and localities was so strong that the possibility of an end to the confederation was very real. We therefore begin by examining the colonial condition and the nature of the struggle against the British. This will allow an appreciation of the manner in which the constitutional settlement contained radical sentiments. We then turn our attention to the way in which the national question was resolved.

The undoubted cultural, economic, and political differences within British North America — between the Puritans of Massachusetts, the distressed cavaliers of Virginia, the Quakers of the Delaware, and the Scots-Irish of Pennsylvania and the West[1] — were counterbalanced by a series of uniformities. The first and most obvious were linguistic and cultural. Whatever their differences, the colonists were nonetheless English in both language and custom. The importance of a shared religion can also scarcely be exaggerated. The colonists were over-

---

[1] D. H. Fischer, *Albion's Seed: Four British Folkways in North America* (Oxford: Oxford University Press, 1989). A major thesis of this book concerns the continuing power of the four cultures identified.

whelmingly Protestant, and many had fled from religious persecution. Of course, this did not in itself necessarily lead to toleration: some groups — especially the Puritans of the Northeast — zealously sought to impose their own uniformities. But a series of forces mitigated against the emergence of permanent religious schisms. For one thing, the Quakers of Pennsylvania and the Virginians were relatively tolerant of other Protestant sects. For another, where intolerance was greatest, the openness of the society allowed dissidents to depart to build their own versions of Jerusalem, hence avoiding war with one another. Furthermore, in a decentralized agrarian society where self-sufficiency was compulsory, there was an inevitable movement away from orthodoxy to independent judgment in matters of faith. The Great Awakening of the early eighteenth century saw what was to become a recurring pattern within American life, namely, the stimulation of popular religious enthusiasm at the expense of the hierarchies of established churches.[2]

The political economy of the colonists exhibited further common features. This agrarian capitalist world, linked to the British metropole by exports, enjoyed extraordinary success, which was later augmented by increasing commercial enterprise in the ports and cities. Both Adam Smith and Tocqueville commented on the relatively high standard of living and remarkable fertility of British North America.[3] It is not correct to

---

[2] P. V. Bonomi, *Under the Cope of Heaven* (New York: Oxford University Press, 1986), and D. S. Lovejoy, *Religious Enthusiasm in the New World* (Cambridge: Harvard University Press, 1985), offer accounts of the Great Awakening. R. Wuthnow, *Sharing the Journey: Support Groups and America's New Quest for Community* (New York: Free Press, 1994), describes the democratizing effect of contemporary America's religious revivals.

[3] A. Smith, *An Inquiry into the Nature and Causes of the Wealth of Nations* (reprint, Oxford: Oxford University Press, 1976), 88, 373, 374–75, 497–98; A. de Tocqueville, *Democracy in America* (reprint, New York: Anchor

suggest, however, as do some of the theorists of American exceptionalism, that there was in consequence an egalitarian distribution of wealth and income.[4] To the contrary, colonial life witnessed the emergence of a potential upperclass. Large plantations dominated the South, while descendants of the early settlers in the North made huge commercial fortunes. In 1670, an estimated one-third of all wealth was held by 5 percent of the population. A century later, 3 percent owned one-quarter of the wealth, and around the time Tocqueville was extolling equality as the central aspect of the American experience, wealth was distributed more disproportionately than at any time before or since: 1 percent of the population owned more than a third of all wealth, while the top 10 percent held not less than four-fifths. Nor was there any great social mobility: in this era, less than 2 percent of the rich were not born rich.[5]

This is, of course, but one side of the matter. "One of the most striking features of class in America is the widespread disbelief in its existence."[6] We will discuss this remarkable ideology at more length later, but note here that the inability of

---

Books, 1969), 408–13. See D. Potter, *People of Plenty: Economic Abundance and the American Character* (Chicago: University of Chicago Press, 1954), for an account of the ways in which abundance has shaped American life.

[4] The leading figures of this school include L. Hartz, D. Bell, R. Hofstader, and S. M. Lipset, whose *American Exceptionalism: A Double-Edged Sword* (New York: Norton, 1996) masterfully summarizes the claims advanced. We comment on the interpretation of this school in the Conclusion.

[5] For these figures, see E. Pessen, "The Egalitarian Myth and the American Social Reality: Wealth, Mobility, and Equality in the 'Era of the Common Man,'" in E. Pessen, ed., *The Many-faceted Jacksonian Era* (Westport, Conn.: Greenwood Press, 1977), and "Status and Class in America," in L. S. Luedtke, ed., *Making America: The Society and Culture of the United States* (Chapel Hill: University of North Carolina Press, 1992).

[6] Pessen, "Status and Class in America," 362.

the early American gentry to gain genuine deference was due in part to the fact that in America — so different from Europe at this point — elite status derived primarily from mercantile success. Even in the South, aristocratic Virginian planters traced their ancestry to tradespeople who had purchased their nobility. A known history of achieved status undercut any elite claims to innate superiority and lessened the potential for class warfare. Furthermore, as Turner noted, the availability of new lands to the west "did indeed furnish a new field of opportunity, a gate of escape from the bondage of the past."[7] American settler-farmers thus bore some resemblance to nomads in being able to get up and move, and were therefore resistant to control by any establishment.[8] All this deserves summary: for Americans, success existed both in fact and as aspiration.

A shared racism also underwrote early American unity. There may very well be, as Orlando Patterson has argued for many years, a deep connection between the concepts of freedom and slavery.[9] Just as the idea of freedom arose in the slave societies of Greece, so, too, was liberty appreciated in early America in counterpoise to its opposite: "among whites of all orders slavery established a kind of equality."[10] Recent schol-

---

[7] F. J. Turner, "The Significance of the Frontier in American History," reprinted in J. Hall, ed., *Forging the American Character* (New York: Holt, Rinehart and Winston, 1971), 63.

[8] Even after the closure of the frontier at the end of the nineteenth century, Americans continued to exercise the option of escape through social and geographical mobility. For a classic statement of this argument, see G. W. Pierson, "The M-Factor in American History," *American Quarterly* 14 (1962): 275–89.

[9] O. Patterson, *Freedom* (New York: Basic Books, 1991). Cf. E. S. Morgan, *American Slavery, American Freedom: The Ordeal of Colonial Virginia* (New York: Norton, 1975).

[10] R. Middlekauff, *The Glorious Cause: The American Revolution, 1763–1789* (Oxford: Oxford University Press, 1982), 606. We should note, how-

arship has come to consider the dispossession of Native Americans as equally racist. Because property was recognized only in the form of agricultural land, settlers were legally permitted and even encouraged to use force and fraud to dislocate the aboriginal inhabitants. Appropriation of native land was also excused, by John Locke, on the grounds of efficiency:

> For I aske whether in the wild woods and uncultivated wast of America left to Nature, without any improvement, tillage or husbandry, a thousand acres will yield the needy and wretched inhabitants as many conveniences of life as ten acres of equally fertile land doe in Devonshire where they are well cultivated?[11]

Believing dispossession to be the replacement of savagery by civilization, and viewing slavery as a confirmation of the natural superiority of whites over blacks, the vast majority of white Americans were solidly united in maintaining their innate right to dominate and disinherit other races.

These unifying aspects were amplified by British intervention. It is true that the logistics of early modern communications meant that control of the colonies from Westminster was

---

ever, that slavery and indentured servitude of whites (and some blacks) were for some time coexistent in the colonies, and that the two conditions were not easily distinguishable. Only at the end of the seventeenth century did skin pigmentation become the primary mechanism for assigning persons to the unfree labor category, which was decisively shifted from redeemable indentured servitude to absolute slavery. See R. Williams, *Hierarchical Structures and Social Value: The Creation of Black and Irish Identities in the United States* (Cambridge: Cambridge University Press, 1990), chaps. 3 and 4.

[11] J. Locke, *Two Treatises of Government*, ed. P. Laslett (reprint, Cambridge: Cambridge University Press, 1991), second treatise, sec. 37, cited in J. Tully, *Strange Multiplicity* (Cambridge: Cambridge University Press, 1995), 75.

necessarily sketchy and occasional. Still, the crown did attempt to rein in the effective independence of this diverse and decentralized new society—about which, however, it knew next to nothing. Considerable popular resentment was aroused by the British attempt to undermine Puritan hegemony in Massachusetts and by the Proclamation of 1763, which threatened to limit expansion to the West; more important, the interests of local gentry everywhere in the colonies were threatened by the possibility of blocked social mobility should London start to send out large numbers of its own governing agents. What came to matter most, however, was taxation. British military success in the late eighteenth century was bought at considerable financial cost, and the central state sought to share the burden of defense by asking for what were in fact rather limited contributions from the colonies.[12] This was timed inopportunely. Fiscal extraction tends to be accepted when the necessity for protection by a state is obvious. The very amplitude of the British victories in the French and Indian Wars undermined the rationale for taxation. Meanwhile, the sugar interests of the Caribbean used their great influence in the English parliament to enact duties aimed at retaining their own domination of trade: the perceived unfairness and exploitative nature of these taxes outraged the colonists.

The colonial opponents of British demands did not initially see themselves as anything other than British. They were firmly committed to the British political tradition's stress on individual liberties and rights. The refusal of Britain to pay attention to the old maxims of canon law and parliamentary tradition ("no taxation without representation," "what concerns all must be decided by all") was seen as treachery to its best

---

[12] J. Brewer, *The Sinews of War: War, Money and the English State, 1688–1783* (New York: Knopf, 1989) offers a marvelous account of the finances of the British state.

self and a betrayal of the rights of all free-born Englishmen. In consequence, the rebels at the outset sought to awaken the crown to its duties. But British intransigence soon led to more radical protestations, first about the Rights of Man and then about the need for an independent popular government.

Independence did not result wholly from the actions of the patriots. While they fought hard and well, the liberty and decentralization of the colonial forces did much to undermine their military effectiveness, as generals bickered over strategy and citizen-soldiers refused to obey officers not from their own town, or simply left the Continental army when their short term of enlistment was up, satisfied that they had done their duty. What mattered more was the fundamental blunder of the metropole. Wars are often won by diplomats, whose provision of allies does much to allow for the concentration of forces. In this case, Britain fought without allies, and felt it necessary to keep large forces in reserve at home to deal with any French incursion into Ireland. This left its colonial army greatly weakened, largely reliant on Hessian mercenaries to do their fighting for them. When these troops were defeated, the British had no recourse except to accede to American independence.

After Washington's great victory, the British retired, leaving the victors with no central government whose institutions could be taken over to transform social relations.[13] Many radicals were glad of this; protective of their hard-won freedom, they wished to have nothing to do with a central state, fearing it would be an arena for the despotism of an upper class. Escaping the state altogether by moving West seemed a more

[13] In this sense, the independence movement does not fit the usual definition of revolution as a fundamental transformation of social relations achieved by means of a takeover of state power. On this matter, see T. Skocpol, *States and Social Revolution* (Cambridge: Cambridge University Press, 1979). Cf. J. Goldstone, *Revolution and Rebellion in the Early Modern World* (Berkeley: University of California Press, 1991).

attractive option. Still, this anarchistic strain was partially offset by urbanites of the North, who believed a state was a practical necessity.[14] More important, the formation of a state was also favored by the respectable propertied elite. There were several reasons for this.

During the war, the gentry had been forced to encourage mass military mobilization — an accomplishment made easier by the fact that many ordinary Americans were already in the habit of personally defending themselves against American Indians. "Everybody here was a bit of a soldier, no one completely so. War was conducted without a professional army, without generals, and even without 'soldiers' in the strict European sense."[15] Although they were often not very well disciplined, the conscripts were experienced in guerrilla warfare; they were also excellent marksmen, and in the lightweight, quick-loading, locally manufactured "Pennsylvania" rifle they had the best weapon of the time. During the war, the militiamen had plenty of opportunity to hone their military skills. Violence was extensive, especially in the first phase of the conflict, with military proceedings taking on the character of a civil war. Control of the means of coercion by the citizenry meant that anti-aristocratic legislation, such as abolition of primogeniture and entail, was achieved very soon after the war. The refusal to countenance an upper house in Pennsylvania seemed further to suggest that the class status of the gentry might not be secure. Added to this was a good deal of corruption at the level of the states and an utter incapacity to make international treaties — a matter of real importance given the continuing presence at the time of British and Spanish em-

[14] G. Nash, *The Urban Crucible: The Northern Seaports and the Origins of the American Revolution* (Cambridge: Harvard University Press, 1986).

[15] D. Boorstin, "Defensive Warfare and Naïve Diplomacy," in R. Boorstin, ed., *The Daniel J. Boorstin Reader* (New York: Modern Library, 1995), 86.

pires. Finally, dispossession of the gentry had also been wide-spread: Loyalists in America were five times more likely to flee than were aristocrats in revolutionary France — which is to say that the United States was born in the midst of a severe dose of political cleansing, very often directed at the wealthy. This naturally exacerbated the anxiety of the revolutionary elite about the dangers of popular rule.[16] In these circumstances, the men of substance of the Continental Congress came to feel that the establishment of a national government was of paramount importance.

Most of the delegates sent by the states to discuss the question of national unity at Philadelphia were notables, members of the establishment who chose, revealingly, to discuss matters in private, free from public scrutiny.[17] If this allowed for a centralizing, elitist voice such as that of Alexander Hamilton to be raised, most members, and in particular James Madison, were extremely practical — and thus well aware that any constitution would need popular support in order to be ratified. Let us

[16] R. Palmer, *The Age of the Democratic Revolution* (Princeton, N.J.: Princeton University Press, 1959), vol. 1, pp. 188–202, cited in M. Mann, *The Sources of Social Power*, vol. 2, *The Rise of Classes and Nation-States, 1760–1914* (Cambridge: Cambridge University Press, 1993), 150. We have learned a great deal from Mann's analysis of the American Revolution. It is very noticeable that some of the Founders were disquieted by the blanket attack on those members of their class who had chosen the wrong side, wishing to distinguish between naive Loyalists and a smaller number who had actively done evil to the Patriot cause. For the views of Hamilton and Jay in 1783, see R. B. Morris, *Witnesses at the Creation* (New York: New American Library, 1985), 41–42. Note also that the Revolution did not level out economic differences; to the contrary, "wealth tended to become more unequally distributed after the Revolution than it had been before" (Pessen, "Status and Class in America"), 368.

[17] For a sociological portrait of the Founders, see M. Mann and J. Stephens, "American Revolutionaries: Social Class and the Founding Fathers" (unpublished manuscript, 1991).

consider the critical provisions of the Constitution, and then turn to the key political institutions that developed in consequence.

At the convention, little time was spent discussing property. The Framers themselves were property owners who wished their rights to be protected. There was no challenge to this because those who lacked property both hoped and believed that they would be able to acquire it—a view made slightly more reasonable at the time by the way in which fortunes had been lost and gained during the war, both in commerce and as the result of dispossession. Opportunities offered by the frontier also made Americans believe that they could achieve wealth, that property was something to be sought, not limited. The end result was simple: property rights became a key principle in the grammar of American politics.

These scholar-gentlemen decided as well to separate church from state, that is, to allow a right to believe while taking religious issues off the political agenda. The influence of Virginia at this point was significant. That state had long had a tradition of religious tolerance verging on disinterest, due in part to the spatial decentralization of their plantation society and in part to the moderate views of the freeholder elites, who had come to the New World less to escape religious persecution than to pursue their pragmatic economic interests. In this context, members of any religious sect were welcome to practice in the commonwealth so long as they proved themselves to be "men of good will" rather than zealots. As one Virginian gentleman wrote in 1767:

> I think I Could Live in Love & Peace, with a good Man of any of the various Sects Christians; Nor do I perceive any necessity for differing or quarrelling with a Man, because he may not Think exactly as I do. I might as well quarrel with him for not being of the same Size or Complexion

with myself. For the different Operations of the Mind are not to be accounted for.[18]

The Virginian attitude of tolerance, combined with the gradual dispersal of the fanatical religious communities of New England and the divinely mandated open-mindedness of the Quakers, provided a grounding for the uniquely American attitude toward religion: all citizens can choose a belief and practice it, so long as they do not interfere with the beliefs and practices of others. By refusing to establish a state religion and giving each individual the right of religious freedom, the Founders ensured that religious disputes would not, as so often happened in Europe, layer themselves on top of other sources of conflict.[19] In this system, there is little occasion for churchly challenges to state authority, while movement among sects and the tendency for their interests to clash makes it hard to polarize society along any single religious dimension.[20] This model came to define the American experience of religion: the vast majority are believers, but no one faith predominates, and new religions are continually being born. The appearance of millenarian awakenings and local charismatic cults that has long been characteristic of American religious life has been a small price to pay for the stability secured by this arrangement.

If the Founders agreed on religion and property rights, they

---

[18] These are the views of Col. William Green, cited by D. Boorstin, "From Country Squire to Planter Capitalist," in R. Boorstin, *Daniel J. Boorstin Reader*, p. 45.

[19] The most powerful appreciation of the radicalizing effect of the superimposition of conflicts remains R. Dahrendorf, *Class and Class Conflict in Industrial Society*, rev. ed. (Stanford: Stanford University Press, 1959).

[20] The first and most brilliant appreciation of this point was that of Adam Smith, who, in an argument interestingly directed against his friend David Hume, insisted that competition between many sects would diminish fanaticism. Smith, *Wealth of Nations*, 792–93. Cf. D. Martin, *A General Theory of Secularization* (Oxford: Blackwell, 1978).

were far less unified on the form the state should take. The first crucial point concerned the very possibility of a republican union. Traditional republicans, following Machiavelli, insisted that virtue could be created only in a state of limited size, an argument that spoke strongly against the union.[21] But Madison brilliantly propounded two arguments, drawn from Montesquieu, to suggest that size was no obstacle to stability. The first was a sort of left-handed, sour grapes theory, akin in spirit to the view that a market of religions would diminish fanaticism. Political factions *would* proliferate in an incompletely virtuous world, but their very pluralism would inevitably lead, through a process of mutual stalemate, to political stability.[22] The second argument stressed that representation would allow for the voice of the people to be heard — but in a suitably moderate, modulated form. At this point Madison's views are best seen as addressing the problem of containing popular enthusiasm. There was substantial fear amongst the elite that the state, much though it was needed, might become a danger were it to fall into the intemperate hands of an impassioned people. These fears can be particularly clearly seen in Madison's comments on the requirement for a senate. After noting that an upper house would protect the people against its rulers, he went on to endorse an upper house on the opposite ground that it would prevent the people making legislation on the basis of their own "transient impressions":

> Another reflection equally becoming a people on such an occasion, wd. be that they themselves, as well as a numerous body of Representatives, were liable to err also, from fickleness and passion. A necessary fence agst. this

---

[21] J. Shklar, "Montesquieu and the New Republicanism," in G. Bock, Q. Skinner and M. Viroli, eds., *Machiavelli and Republicanism* (Cambridge: Cambridge University Press, 1992).

[22] The classic statement of this view is the tenth letter of *The Federalist*.

danger would be to select a portion of enlightened citizens, whose limited number and firmness might seasonably interpose agst. impetuous counsels.[23]

The executive veto would equally serve to control passionate majorities. Added to these mechanisms for control of the masses was the division of powers within the legislature and its separation from the executive, together with a supreme court to ensure dominance by the rule of law.

Although the Founders were very often men of considerable sophistication, it would be a mistake to suggest that the constitutional settlement was a brilliant exercise in abstract political theory. For one thing, the implicit sociology of the Founders was quite often wrong. The expectation that large constituencies would bring "the better sort" to serve as representatives, for example, was shortly to be proved quite false. For another, key elements were the result less of careful reasoning than of political necessity and compromise. Most significant, small states fearing the domination of the great combined with southern states wishing to protect slavery to ensure that the American state would be more confederal than centralized. In sum, the problem of national unity was but half-solved, and the viability of a country that contained very different interests remained an ongoing issue.

The Constitution was — and is — a complicated affair, and it gained ratification only by a slim margin. Its success depended heavily on the way in which it would be made to operate at the start. From the point of view of its creators, the early years seemed unpromising, and Washington's remarks in his Farewell Address were full of anxieties about the dangers of faction and disunion. Hamilton sought to overcome the tendency to

[23] Quoted in M. Farrand, ed., *The Records of the Federal Convention of 1787* (New Haven: Yale University Press, 1937), vol. 1, 422.

disintegration by his plans for a powerful and centralized state, modeled after Britain and thus possessed of financial and military means. But this program proved anathema to southern planters, not least to Jefferson and to Madison, whose agrarian interests and republican ideals led them to be enamored of a more decentralized, bucolic view of America's future.

This split within the elite in the early years of the republic might have sparked a civil war, especially since the Alien and Sedition Act of 1798 was in part designed for use against political opposition.[24] But in comparison to the concentrated military strength of Virginia, Hamilton and the Federalists had no really effective coercive means at their disposal. Meanwhile, Jefferson and then Jackson appealed to the people against the Federalist attempt to create a new central establishment; the people responded favorably, displaying the same anti-authoritarianism they had shown in the Revolutionary War.[25] The result was the extension of the suffrage to virtually all white males by the 1830s, which ensured that politics in America would be popular: henceforth, politicians would have to mingle and communicate with the masses in order to gain their electoral support. Even more crucial was the development in the United States of a stable dual party system, in which authority was surrendered simply as a matter of course by the party in power after a lost election, with every expectation that it could be won back again at a later date. One catalyst for this remarkable system of conflict regulation, so essential to the country's long-term political stability, was the fact that a grow-

---

[24] R. Hofstadter, *The Idea of a Party System: The Rise of Legitimate Opposition in the United States, 1780–1840* (Berkeley: University of California Press, 1969).

[25] For a superb local exemple of the defeat of an attempted new class system, see A. Taylor, *William Cooper's Town: Power and Persuasion on the Frontier of the Early American Republic* (New York: Knopf, 1995).

ing economy meant that there were many avenues of social mobility available outside the arena of politics. One did not need to be a political actor to be a success. Another factor was that Jefferson did much of Hamilton's work, most obviously in the Louisiana Purchase, which added such huge resources to the federal government. All this is to say that a considerable measure of elite unity was recreated, as was evident in the hidden pact not to allow slavery to become a political issue.[26] Consideration of the breakdown of that agreement is the next issue to be confronted.

[26] M. Shefter, *Political Parties and the State* (Princeton, N.J.: Princeton University Press, 1994), 11.

The national question

The Civil War was less the breaking of a common, firmly established mold than the logical development of the tensions present at the moment of foundation. These tensions were evident, for example, when the northern states almost split from the Union in 1814 in opposition to the federal policy that had brought war with Great Britain, their own natural economic partner. It was only in the middle of the nineteenth century, as the result of the Civil War, that the definitive, if imperfect, step to a unified nation-state was finally taken. This should not surprise us. Mass mobilization for military purposes has been the greatest builder of national sentiment everywhere; for example, in France peasants became Frenchmen, we have been reliably told, only as the result of the conscription imposed after the defeat of 1870–1871.[1]

That there were fundamental differences between regional ways of life was apparent in the accommodations inscribed in the Constitution. If the absence of a strong central structure appealed to many states nervous of political hegemony of any sort, the situation of the South, dependent as it was on slavery, effectively mandated states' rights. Further, there had long been a deep ambivalence about race. For instance, Thomas Jefferson believed it would be better if America were united and white; but he also held that intelligence and ability varied by skin color — making slavery justified as long as his preferred option, returning blacks to Africa, had not been put into effect.[2] The Constitution certainly contained a series of provisions that recognized the workings of slavery, though many leading voices hoped that these would be temporary if repatria-

[1] E. Weber, *Peasants into Frenchmen* (Stanford: Stanford University Press, 1976).

[2] W. Freehling, "The Founding Fathers and Slavery," in his *The Reintegration of American History: Slavery and the Civil War* (New York: Oxford University Press, 1994).

tion took place — or, if slavery were abolished, an option then attractive to very few. At least three of these deserve to be noted. First, Article I, Section 2, counted each slave as three-fifths of a person when calculating southern representation in the House of Representatives — a formula that benefited the North by diminishing representation from the South. Second, Article I, Section 9, Paragraph 5 prohibited imposition of an export tax, thus effectively preventing interference with the cotton sector. Third, Article IV, Section 2, Paragraph 3, was, ironically, designed to limit the legislative rights of states: fugitive slaves were to retain their status as property, subject to being reclaimed by their owners from any state.

Although the implicit constitutional legitimization of slavery mattered a great deal, America was bound together quite as much by a set of informal bargains. To begin with, the political elite was almost completely united in its determination not to allow the question of slavery to become an issue of public life. Both Whigs and Democrats were national parties, and they found it in their interest to create gag rules in Congress to exclude an issue that could only lead to the diminution of their status. Furthermore, the South was not marginalized in political life; to the contrary, it provided most of the national leaders throughout the antebellum period. Finally, the sectional balance of the federal system was preserved time and again by compromise, habitually as a result of the South's threat to secede. The informal agreement to admit one slave state for every new free state was maintained in 1820 and in 1832; the rather different compromise of 1850, allowing the populace of new territories to decide the matter, proved to be a miscalculation on the part of the South.

Obviously, both the formal and informal means of bridging the gaps that existed between the different worlds of North and South eventually came to naught. To explain this, it is necessary to chart the way in which changes in the relations between the political economies of the two regions, especially in the light of the new interests of the West, led to a novel structure of political opportunity.[3] To such structural consideration must be added, however, appreciation of the impact of American anti-slavery sentiment.

What is most noticeable initially about the South was its extraordinary prosperity. The introduction of the cotton gin enabled cotton cultivation throughout the South just as demand from the mills of Lancashire began its enormous increase. Thus was born the boom period of an export-led, free trade economy, whose wealth did much to enrich the North as well as the South. Prior to the Civil War, there was no real sign that this economy was faltering in any serious way. It is true that soil exhaustion led to the cessation of cotton growing in the Upper South, but compensation for this was found in specialization: old areas of cotton production became centers for the breeding of slaves, while production itself moved to the Deep South. Yet, despite its commercial success, the South was scarcely a calm and self-confident social world. The charges of northern abolitionists, such as William Lloyd Garrison, that slaveholding was a dreadful sin were deeply resented as threats to southern liberty and as insults to southern honor.[4] When the abolitionist Massachusetts senator Charles Sumner described slavery as a harlot in 1856, he was beaten almost to death by

---

[3] The contours of the explanation that follow have been molded by B. Moore, *Social Origins of Dictatorship and Democracy* (Boston: Beacon Press, 1966), chap. 3. Cf. R. Keohane, "Associationist American Development, 1776–1860: Economic Growth and Political Disintegration," in J. Ruggie, ed., *The Antinomies of Interdependence* (New York: Columbia University Press, 1983).

[4] B. Wyatt-Brown, *Southern Honor: Ethics and Behavior in the Old South* (New York: Oxford University Press, 1982).

an outraged southern congressman — an act greeted with de-
light in the South.[5] In response to northern accusations, southern ideology, especially in South Carolina, came to stress the
benign paternalism of a hierarchical elite responsible for poor
whites as well as for slaves. This ideological development had
about it an air of defensive aggression that derived more from
anxiety and a fear of violation than from self-confidence.[6]

While the South was solidifying its identity as agricultural
and racist, the North was experiencing fundamental transformations, as its economy was beginning to be subject to the
forces of industrialization. This was made possible by a revolution in transportation that allowed for increasing specialization
and for urbanization. Even though the export of cotton played
a vital role in the North's prosperity, diversification was nonetheless taking place into textiles, iron and steel, and manufacturing. Still, northern industrialists felt themselves to be at the
mercy of more advanced industrial countries, and sought —
particularly in times of depression — for protective tariffs for
their infant industries; the tariff issue thus became a sharp
point of contention between the regions. This was a matter of
consequence since the South feared that any increase in federal power might eventually be used against slavery. Equally
important, the North was also attracting significant immigration, which reached a peak in the years immediately preceding
the Civil War. Such immigration was novel in bringing Catholics from Ireland and Germany into the United States, and it
affected America unevenly given that virtually none went to

---

[5] P. Boller, *Congressional Anecdotes* (New York: Oxford University Press
1991), 46–48.

[6] Freehling, *Reintegration of American History*, esp. chaps. 5 and 6.
R. Nisbett and D. Cohen, *Culture of Honor: The Psychology of Violence in
the South* (Boulder, Colo.: Westview, 1996), offer reasons for the high
rates of violence and murder that continue to prevail in the South.

the South.[7] The popular response to this in the North was often nativist, as in the rise of the "Know-Nothing" American party. But economic development and rapid population increase was bound to enhance the North's political power in the long run.

The opening of the Great Plains made the West nothing less than a third distinctive political economy. In purely economic terms, the West mattered both for the agricultural products — hogs, corn, wheat — it provided for northern cities and for the market it furnished for the manufacturing industries of the North. But it was the political aspect that was crucial. The West became the bastion of the Free-Soilers, that is, of independent small farmers — and, of course, of those who dreamed of owning such farms — who were convinced that the extension of slavery would ruin their life chances. Such people revered independence and were quite obviously out of tune with the paternalist ideology of the southern planter aristocracy.

Comparative historical sociology has made it entirely apparent that there is no automatic and necessary link between capitalism and freedom.[8] To the contrary, capitalism has often flourished in combination with authoritarian rule — indeed, some of its forms have depended upon tyranny for the provision of a disciplined labor force.[9] In principle, then, it was possible for there to have been some accommodation between the industrialists of the North and the planters of the South. However, two conditions were lacking that might have done a

---

[7] To this day, of all the regions of the United States, only the South lacks a substantial Catholic population.

[8] This is a complex question. Capitalism and authoritarianism fit best when a state seeks to catch up with the heavy industrialization of its neighbors. It is rather harder to run late industrial society along authoritarian lines.

[9] Moore, *Social Origins*; D. Rueschemeyer, E. Stephens, and J. Stephens, *Capitalist Development and Democracy* (Chicago: University of Chicago Press, 1992).

great deal to forge such a political alliance.[10] In the first place, the industrialists of the North had no special need for an authoritarian state: labor was not particularly unruly, partially because the influx of immigrants provided a renewable pool of new and docile workers. Calculation on the part of industrialists at this point was, we shall see later, essentially correct: a set of institutional factors meant that American capitalism was able to establish its authority without the need to embrace an authoritarian regime. However, accommodation might still have been forced upon the industrialists and planters had they been faced by a common threat to their survival. Geopolitical menaces to the state most certainly had that consequence within Wilhelmine Germany. But America was effectively an island, as Tocqueville had noted, and this allowed for the full playing out of conflict between different political economies with a minimum of external intervention.[11]

But these two factors are really beside the point. For the North had a better political option than accommodation with the South. This was to forge an alliance with the West. Territorial extension of the United States had undermined the political vision of Jefferson and Jackson. That vision assumed a coalition of planters *with* small farmers—something that seemed to be cemented by Andrew Jackson's destruction of the Bank of the United States and by continuing populist attacks on an eastern establishment, portrayed as an obstacle to self-sufficiency and manly individualism. But in 1854 white males of limited means and large dreams left the Democrats—and the Whigs, too— because they were appalled that the Kansas-Nebraska Act allowed for the introduction of slavery into the western territories. These voters understood that the expansion of slavery would ruin their hopes for financial independence.

[10] Moore, *Social Origins*, 140–41.

[11] Tocqueville, *Democracy in America*, 278.

Although they left originally to enter the American party, whose numbers shot up dramatically, their interests soon came to find stable expression with the Republicans. Born in 1854, this party proved itself capable of winning a presidential election a mere six years later. The essential bargain making for Republican political success was summed up in the electoral slogan of 1860: "Vote yourself a farm — vote yourself a tariff." The alliance of western farmers and northern industrialists was joined as well by recent immigrants, whose loyalty the Republicans gained by downplaying nativist sentiment, so as to move away from the Jeffersonian concept of an Anglo-America to a more encompassing vision of Euro-America.[12]

The Republican victory of 1860 created crisis because for the first time a president had been elected completely without support from the South. The country was effectively divided, and passions ran high on both sides. Lincoln himself was the very model of caution, insisting time and again that he had no desire, capacity, or intention to interfere with the South's peculiar institution. No real heed was paid to his reassurances, let alone to the fact that he, too, favored the return of blacks to Africa. Southerners instead realized that Lincoln regarded the moral principles of the Declaration of Independence, rather than the mere political accord of the Constitution, as America's foundation stone, and consequently paid attention to his famous "house divided" speech, which had argued that restriction of slavery would inevitably end in its "ultimate extinction."[13] Nationalism often thrives on fear, and, led by South

---

[12] This is the view of M. Lind, *The Next American Nation: The New Nationalism and the Fourth American Revolution* (New York: Free Press, 1995).

[13] Freehling, *Reintegration of American History*, describes how that extinction might have come about: "Lincoln might have developed a southern wing of his party, and Lincoln's proposed policy of removing blacks from

Carolina, extremists in the South agreed that this was the time to take a stand. The initial secession of a mere seven states expanded, as South Carolinians had expected, when the North's strong response to the assault on Fort Sumter forced the less warlike Southerners to realize they would either have to join the Confederacy or else be obliged to fire on their fellows.

As with all great historical issues, debate continues as to the fundamental stake at issue in the war. There can be no doubt but that Lincoln regarded the secession as a rebellion, and his own paramount objective was saving the Union rather than immediately destroying slavery — as was so clearly evident in his refusal to insist on emancipation of slaves within "slave states" that fought for the Union.[14] Still, it was slavery that lay behind the long history of divisive conflict; it remained the central obstacle to consensus. This is not at all the same thing as saying that there was any generalized enlightenment at work on the side of the Union. It is true that the abolitionist cause had increased in popularity, particularly among women, and that it provided a powerful and inspiring moral voice for eman-

America might have gained more adherents among Upper South voters. In the face of that uncertain climate for its investment in human property, Border South capitalists might have cashed in their slaves at Lower South auctions. Such sales southward were always the most realistic of the Upper South's black removal scenarios. Eventually, likely well into the twentieth century, some Border South-North fusion might have abolished Lower South slavery, probably by the difficult constitutional amendment process" (135–36).

[14] A. Buchanan, *Secession: The Morality of Political Divorce from Fort Sumter to Lithuania and Quebec* (Boulder, Colo.: Westview, 1991), argues that secession is justified unless a large moral issue is at stake; this leads him to doubt the initial justice of the North's cause, but to see matters quite differently after the Emancipation Proclamation.

cipation, but it remained the voice of a minority.[15] The western interest of Free-Soilers, that is, of white males, was, of course, fundamentally racist, while northern workers hated slavery less as a moral wrong than as a possible threat to their own employment.

Reflection makes us realize that these issues could have been resolved.[16] North and South could have come to some agreement about the role of a larger federal state, especially because the South eventually proved itself keen to accept central investment. That the abolition of slavery does not inevitably lead to armed conflict is demonstrated by the pattern of Brazilian development. In the last analysis, what mattered in the United States was the layering of issues about regional autonomy, divergent cultural attitudes, contrasting modes of production, and the morality of slavery on top one another. A single issue might have been resolved; the superimposition of several caused complex misunderstandings and violent hatreds that made war almost inevitable.

The South was always likely to lose: it lacked both industry and a viable grand strategy.[17] Nonetheless, victory for the Union was by no means easy. It came very much as the result of the forces that Lincoln had marshaled. Immigrants formed the core of the Union forces, while blacks, both as soldiers and as military auxiliaries, made a decisive contribution. But war

---

[15] But see J. McPherson, *For Cause and Comrades: Why Men Fought in the Civil War* (Oxford: Oxford University Press, 1997), for evidence showing that Northerners did gradually become more abolitionist as a result of their wartime experiences.

[16] A. Marx, *Making Race and Nation: A Comparison of the United States, South Africa, and Brazil* (Cambridge: Cambridge University Press, 1998).

[17] It thus falls into a set of cases analyzed in T. V. Paul, *Asymmetric Conflicts: War Initiation by Weaker Powers* (Cambridge: Cambridge University Press, 1994).

needs to be judged, as Clausewitz argued, in political terms. What was victory going to achieve? In this matter, it is useful to recall that greatness in political life is best judged as the capacity to realize as much of one's aims as is politically possible — or, perhaps more accurately, as the ability to expand the bounds of the taken-for-granted in order to achieve new purposes. Lincoln was a master of making such expansions. At the end of the war, it seemed as if he yet might manage to find a middle way between binding up the wounds of the Union — or, as he now preferred to call it, the nation — and permitting blacks a controlled entry into American politics, thus allowing a new birth of freedom in the republic.[18] His assassination was a disaster because it brought lesser men to the fore.

One such was his successor, Andrew Johnson. He reversed the land grants of forty acres per freed slave initiated by Sherman in liberated South Carolina, and spoke scathingly of efforts to "Africanize" the South. The abolitionist elite could not accept this; they sought to impeach Johnson himself, and then imposed radical Reconstruction by returning to military rule states that Johnson had readmitted to the Union. Very great progressive benefits came from some of the policies that were implemented. Blacks made the most of the chance to vote, and soon sent sixteen congressmen and two senators to Washington. Further, between 1863 and 1890, literacy amongst blacks rose from 10 percent to 50 percent, and from 1860 to 1880, the per capita standard of living for blacks increased by 40 percent. But the very rigors of military rule led to resistance, most notably in the form of the Ku Klux Klan, which protested not only against the increased power of blacks, but also against immigrants, Catholics, and federal authority in general — touching deep chords in many Americans both in

---

[18] G. Wills, *Lincoln at Gettysburg* (New York: Simon and Schuster, 1992).

and out of the South. Although the federal state had expanded, partly in order to pay pensions to veterans and widows,[19] it was not as yet powerful enough to stamp out such widespread popular protest. Furthermore, an economic crisis in the North coupled with the distaste of northern industrialists for social policy provisions favoring workers undermined the cohesion of the radicals. The tied presidential election of 1876 signaled a deal that led to the end of Reconstruction. In retreat from the impassioned rhetoric of the war, Americans were glad to indulge in the "materialist barbeque" of the Gilded Age.[20]

We can say, then, that just as the struggle for independence led to a muted revolution, the outcome of the Civil War was marked by a transformation stalled. Obliged to buy off armed southern whites, and tired of sacrifice, the federal government compromised on its principles. Even though slavery was abolished, the South was not wholly defeated in the Civil War. In 1883 the Civil Rights Act of 1875 was struck down by the Supreme Court, and the Jim Crow laws were enacted in 1896, endorsing a "one drop of blood" rule, which did much to underwrite racism thereafter in the United States. Legal segregation in combination with sharecropping meant that bondage replaced slavery. Furthermore, the hopes of the Republican party for votes from the South came to naught: in many states wide-scale disenfranchisement took place, often leaving a mere 30 percent of adult white males as the electorate. Thus was

[19] T. Skocpol, *Protecting Soldiers and Mothers: The Political Origins of Social Policy in the United States* (Cambridge: Harvard University Press, 1992). This was the first indicator that social provision is perfectly acceptable within America's purportedly individualist culture — as long, that is, as welfare is directed to "the deserving."

[20] P. Parish, "Bigger or Better? A Pendulum Theory of American History," in R. Kroes, ed., *The American Identity: Fusion and Fragmentation* (Amsterdam: Amerika Instituut, 1980), 131.

born the Solid South. The first president from the South after the Civil War, Woodrow Wilson, brought Jim Crow segregation to Washington; the next great Democrat, Franklin D. Roosevelt, depended upon his southern electoral base to such an extent that he dared not interfere with its internal workings—making sure that New Deal social policy was designed not to include blacks.[21] It was left to Lyndon Johnson to finally break this alliance, at the cost of condemning his own party to a generation of electoral defeat.

Yet even though the Civil War did not lead to complete emancipation for African Americans, America had nonetheless survived the possibility of genuine destruction. As countries do not like to refight civil wars, especially when they have had a decisive outcome, this has greatly increased the political stability of the nation. In fact, there is no likelihood whatsoever of any popular seccessionist movement arising in the United States, despite rhetoric about "culture wars." We can see this to be the case by reflecting for a moment on the preconditions required for the rise of secessionist movements. The most powerful general theory of nationalism stresses that a high degree of homogeneity provides the foundation required for the successful workings of modern society, and argues further that campaigns for secession result from feelings of humiliation and exclusion among those who are not easily able to participate in the common culture.[22]

Clearly, the United States has become more homogeneous and thus very much more stable since the Civil War. Of

[21] J. Quadagno, *The Transformation of Old Age Security* (Chicago: University of Chicago Press, 1988), and *The Color of Welfare* (New York: Oxford University Press, 1994).

[22] E. Gellner, *Nations and Nationalism* (Oxford: Blackwell, 1983). Cf. J. A. Hall, ed., *The State of the Nation: Ernest Gellner and the Theory of Nationalism* (Cambridge: Cambridge University Press, 1998).

course, the South remains the largest and most culturally singular region of the country, boasting in southern Baptism America's fastest-growing Protestant religion, as well as an idiosyncratic dialect, a lasting musical tradition, strong and characteristic beliefs in honor, gentility, and military valor, marked gender differences, and a high tolerance of violence.[23] Still, these differences have become less and less salient as the South has become a manufacturing center after the relocation of the textile industry during the Second World War, and as its economy has diversified while the Rust Belt of the North has declined. One indicator of a unified economy was the migration of blacks from the South in the middle decades of this century; another is the more recent growth in population in the South, as people from other parts of the country have moved there. This process of cultural integration has been part of a general homogenization taking place in the nation as a whole.[24] Lincoln had sought unification by introducing a holiday for Thanksgiving, and larger nationalizing commemorations soon followed.[25] Much more important in the long run, of course, has been the spread of radio and television, the impact of Madison Avenue's advertising, Hollywood's endless production of dreams, and the introduction of mass spectator sports, all of which have served to further consolidate the na-

[23] For a short outline of southern characteristics see R. Gastril, "Cultural Regions of America,", in L. S. Luedtke, ed., *Making America: The Society and Culture of the United States* (Chapel Hill: University of North Carolina Press, 1992).

[24] For the importance of homogeneity in building a nation, see Gellner, *Nations and Nationalism*.

[25] R. Brubaker, "National Minorities, Nationalizing States and External National Homelands in the New Europe," *Daedalus* 24 (1995): 107–32. For an account of the attempt to nationalize the United States, see L. Spillman, *Nation and Commemoration* (Cambridge: Cambridge University Press, 1997).

tion as a whole and to bring the South more solidly into the mainstream.[26]

As the United States has become more homogeneous, the humiliation and exclusion of regionally distinct groups has lessened. The American Civil War is of interest to theorists of nationalism since it demonstrates that a sense of group aliena- tion leading to secession can have diverse origins. But the clas- sic form remains linguistic, that is, the deep sensation of af- front felt by a linguistic minority when they do not share the lingua franca. Such feelings have led to the breakup of many states, and may soon occasion the destruction of Canada. In the United States, in contrast, the vast majority speak English; in fact, the standard dialect is "more uniform and more univer- sal than any yet known to Western man."[27] The great reluc- tance of Americans even to consider the possibility of a second national language reflects the pervasive sense that shared speech is one of the central mainstays of the society.[28]

One final general point must be made about the coherence of the United States. If humiliation leads to nationalist move-

---

[26] L. Marchand, *Advertising the American Dream* (Berkeley: University of California Press, 1985).

[27] This is partly because Americans, motivated by egalitarianism, have re- sisted elite idiosyncratic pronunciations and have favored the pronuncia- tion of words as they are spelled. See D. Boorstin, "Culture by the Book: The Spelling Fetish," in R. Boorstin, ed., *The Daniel J. Boorstin Reader* (New York: Modern Library, 1995), 61.

[28] A. Wolfe, *One Nation, After All* (New York: Viking, 1998), documents American opposition to a second national language—an attitude that is combined with unquestioned acceptance of a plurality of cultures. One recalls the (perhaps apocryphal) account of a stump speech in a recent election where the candidate insisted that if English was good enough for Jesus Christ then it was good enough for Texas. This attitude was reflected in the recent Californian rejection of a proposition naming Spanish as a second official language. Other binding elements will be considered in the next section.

ments, then it might seem likely that African Americans would make separatist claims — and, indeed, some extremists have done so. But discrimination toward and disadvantage amongst African Americans does not look likely to create any genuinely successful black nationalism.[29] Zionism is perhaps the only case of a successful nationalism that has not based itself on a prior possession of a territorial core. The dispersal of African Americans throughout the United States has effectively deprived them of the option of exit, even though they may lack true voice within the political system.[30]

---

[29] The attempt by Marcus Garvey to find a black homeland in Africa was not successful, though some of his followers did emigrate to Liberia.

[30] "Exit" and "voice" are the categories of A. O. Hirschman, *Exit, Voice and Loyalty* (Cambridge: Harvard University Press, 1970).

The challenge of class

Republican victory led to a tariff regime that lasted unchallenged for half a century, with land grants to railroads doing much to ensure the settlement of the West. Increasing national integration and favorable government policies created new industries, and the huge capitalist fortunes of Rockefeller, Frick, Gould, Vanderbilt, Carnegie, and Morgan. In sum, American society was completely transformed in the second half of the nineteenth century by one of the most dramatic and brutal industrializations in history. Eighty percent of the population was still classified as rural in 1860; this had declined to less than half sometime before entry into the First World War.

This rapid transformation was an enormous shock to Americans, for whom the epitome of the good life was a small farm in a rural community, and who equated freedom with geographical mobility. Once the frontier had closed and cities had been built, it was not surprising to discover widespread popular discontent over the ever greater predominance of factory work and the opulence of the wealthy owners — the fat cats living up on the hill. Our concern here is with the challenge to industrial capitalism that came from below in the postbellum years, and with the largely successful efforts of those on the top to control and repress those pressures.

One of the most famous social science treatises about America remains Werner Sombart's *Why Is There No Socialism in the United States?*[1] We begin with a simple answer to this question before turning to the complex response that reveals more about the American experience.

Of course, Sombart's question prejudges matters by presuming socialism to be the norm, the natural response to industrial capitalism. A moment's thought should make us doubt this. There have in fact been very few socialist working classes in

---

[1] W. Sombart, *Why Is There No Socialism in the United States?* (London: Macmillan, 1976).

the history of the world. Russian workers before 1914 were perhaps the most radical socialists of all, becoming at times genuine revolutionaries prepared to seize power through direct action.[2] Somewhat less radical was the working class of Wilhelmine Germany, which supported both industrial and political strategies within the Social Democratic party—but which ended up as respectable and reformist rather than revolutionary.[3] Comparative historical sociology has explained these outliers of radical feeling as the result of the superimposition of political repression on top of industrial conflict. It was impossible for workers in Russia for a good deal of the time, and for German workers some of the time, to try to better their conditions at the industrial level for a brute reason: the state acted against unions and socialists directly, making it necessary for workers to combat the government in order to make any progress. Social movements gain their character partly as the result of the regimes with which they interact, and in these two cases workers were politicized by their exclusion from political power. Max Weber realized that this was irrational because it was unnecessary. His own proposals for reforming German politics had at their heart the inclusion of the working class in the belief that national sentiment would outweigh socialism—that, to use a different formulation, loyalty would result from the possession of greater voice within the system.[4] His view gains

[2] T. McDaniel, *Autocracy, Capitalism and the Revolution in Russia* (Berkeley: University of California Press, 1988).

[3] J. Kocka, "Problems of Working-Class Formation in Germany," and M. Nolan, "Economic Crisis, State Policy, and Working-Class Formation in Germany, 1870–1900," both in I. Katznelson and A. Zolberg, eds., *Working Class Formation* (Princeton, N.J.: Princeton University Press, 1983); M. Mann, *The Sources of Social Power*, vol. 2, *The Rise of Classes and Nation-States, 1760–1914* (Cambridge: Cambridge University Press, 1993), chaps. 15, 17–18.

[4] M. Weber, "Parliament and Government in a Reconstructed Germany,"

support from the finding that very limited exclusion of workers in Britain led to a labor party rather than a socialist one — to a type of class loyalty rather than to any sort of politicized class consciousness.[5]

It is therefore tempting to see the United States as "exceptional" in lacking socialism altogether because the absence of an old regime made political inclusion so complete.[6] There is a good deal of sense in this. For one thing, loyalty to the established democratic state was increased by participation in the Civil War: workers had successfully fought, after all, for the world's only democracy, and they had done so against the old regime of a southern aristocracy.[7] Another factor mitigating against class warfare was the perceived potential for upward social mobility through hard work that stands at the core of the American dream. America does not have a national aristocracy; elites have always tended to be local, and the ranks of the gentry are — in principle, anyway — permeable.[8] Even today, the most dispossessed Americans continue to believe strongly

---

in Weber, *Economy and Society* (Berkeley: University of California Press, 1978). Again, the terms are taken from A. O. Hirschman, *Exit, Voice and Loyalty* (Cambridge: Harvard University Press, 1978).

[5] R. McKibbin, "Why Was There No Marxism in Great Britain?" *English Historical Review* 99 (1984): 287–331. See also McKibbin's *Ideologies of Class* (Oxford: Oxford University Press, 1990).

[6] This case is made persuasively by S. M. Lipset, "Radicalism or Reformism," in his *Conflict and Consensus* (New Brunswick, N.J.: Transaction Books, 1984).

[7] M. Shefter, *Political Parties and the State* (Princeton, N.J.: Princeton University Press, 1994), 142–43.

[8] This is especially so today given the importance of educational credentials. M. Lind, *The Next American Nation: The New Nationalism and the Fourth American Revolution* (New York: Free Press, 1995), chap. 4, offers a scathing portrayal of the modern overclass, not least of the way in which Ivy League universities reserve places for rich alumnae.

in the possibility of upward mobility, although in actual fact social movement is much more likely to be in the opposite direction.[9] The ever-present American sense of hope is also fueled by the democratizing uniformity of dress and discourse, and the casualness and absence of deference that are so characteristic of American public culture. Such symbolic expressions of equality have a strong effect on subjective perceptions of difference, in spite of invidious objective economic inequities. These aspects of American society are in part responsible for the fact that only a small minority of workers have ever been involved in political activity. Even though the first working-class parties in the modern world were formed in the United States in the 1830s, the appeal of Horatio Alger has probably always been greater than that of Karl Marx.

Though correct as far as it goes, this very general view in the end distorts. For class sentiment in postbellum America did not initially differ all that much from that of European societies. The degree of union density did not lag behind that of Europe, and to this must be added a strike rate that was probably rather greater, with unions capable of very strong militancy, as was seen in the Railroad Strike of 1877, the general strike of 1886 for shorter working hours, and the Homestead and Pullman strikes of the early 1890s. The fact that American capitalism witnessed a process of corporate mergers after 1870 led, moreover, to considerable sophistication and range in the arguments against "big business" which was seen as destructive of much-valued American independence.[10] Strikes were also often very directly political, particularly when trying to ensure the local adoption of federal legislation. For instance, the

---

[9] K. Newman, *Falling from Grace: The Experience of Downward Mobility in the American Middle Class* (New York: Free Press, 1988).

[10] This is part of a more general American dislike of anything "big," including "big unions" and "big government."

meeting calling for the 1877 general strike in St. Louis re-solved:

> That, as the condition of an immense number of people now forced in idleness, and the great suffering for the nec-essaries of life caused by the monopoly in the hands of the capitalists, appeals strongly to all industrial classes for prompt action, therefore, to avoid bloodshed or violence, we recommend a general strike of all branches of industry for eight hours as a day's work, and we call on the legisla-ture for the immediate enactment of an eight hour law, and the enforcement of a severe penalty for its violation, and that the employment of all children under fourteen years of age be prohibited.[11]

American cultural legacies of masculine independence and a hatred of authoritarian control exacerbated resentment towards the new industrial conglomorates. This led to the expansion of the Order of the Knights of Labor, whose membership reached 703,000 by the summer of 1886. An unusual and very Ameri-can element of its organizational structure was the "mixed as-sembly," which small employers could join on the grounds that they were productive workers rather than predatory finan-ciers. But the rapid decline in membership by the end of the decade suggests that many members were looking for a more radical class position, which some soon found in the American Railway Union, led by socialist Eugene Debs. Finally, one should note that workers were often prepared to exercise vio-lence, with organizations such as the Molly Maguires and the Industrial Workers of the World being quite willing to act out-side laws they took to be repressive.

So the hold of capitalism was not so complete in the United States that workers found it impossible to imagine any alterna-

---

[11] Shefter, *Political Parties and the State*, 119.

tive; nor was political inclusion so effective as to rule out alternative forms of political organization. In a nutshell, America was not yet "exceptional" in terms of its class structure. But it soon became so, in large part because of the impact of its institutional legacy.[12] The way in which this happened can be seen by considering in turn the internal divisions within the working class and the repression it faced from the outside so that the rationality of the response of the "business unionism" associated with Samuel Gompers can properly be appreciated.

One major reason for the absence of a workers' party in the United States was the presence of commitments to existing political parties. These made it hard for a workers' party to break the political mold. The secretary of the Bricklayers International Union put the matter forcefully in 1872:

> We have excellent trades' unionists, who are warm democrats and zealous republicans . . . and who are ready to point with suspicion to every movement on our part towards the formation of political organizations. . . . The only way we can be successful with our local and national trades unions is by excluding politics from them.[13]

The bases for these cross-cutting party loyalties were varied. For example, the Irish in New York had been ill served by the Federalist sponsored Alien and Sedition Act, and therefore became staunch Democrats; other workers supported the Republicans in appreciation of the tariffs that protected their jobs. Equally important was the way in which parties had taken to themselves different ethnicities. In this context, it is worth recalling that the political forces that mattered for most workers

---

[12] This formulation is that of Mann, *Sources of Social Power*, vol. 2, p. 638, to whose analysis we are indebted.

[13] Shefter, *Political Parties and the State*, 139.

were local rather than federal, reflecting the decentralization of the American polity and the relative weakness of the federal government. Legislation about an eight-hour day could be passed at the federal level, but this meant little unless the battle for compliance with the law was won locally. Living conditions, particularly housing, depended almost wholly upon favors that could be extracted from the local party machine. The provision of such services meant the creation of loyalties, as workers had to rely on local political operators for their well-being. The attack on political bosses by muckrakers and Progressives at the turn of the century did not destroy party machines; rather, the party bosses learnt to improve their performance, and to provide enough patronage to solidify their bases of support. In any case, the loyalty of workers to these party machines weakened their attachment to any possible workers' alliance.

Ethnicity played an equally important part in strikes. Worker solidarity was greatest in towns marked by ethnic unity, as was the case with the strong unions developed by Polish workers in the steel towns of Pennsylvania. Of course, cross-ethnic alliances were sometimes struck, as in the 1877 St Louis general strike, but in general ethnic diversity undermined working-class cohesion. During the 1871 coal strike in Scranton, for example, Irish and German mine laborers broke ranks with striking Welsh miners in the hope of gaining their jobs, causing irresolvable conflict among the workers.[14] Such divisions were well understood and exploited by employers. As a pamphlet published by the Chamber of Commerce in Hamilton Ohio put it: "Varied labor classes are a benefit to the community for it is a recognized fact that the presence of only a few classes of labor in large numbers in any community tends to

[14] Ibid., 129.

produce a strong labor group that, too often, attracts radical leaders."[15]

A further source of divergence lay in the federated nature of the American political system. Most labor law was enacted at the state level, causing great variation in working conditions across the country. The liberal conditions of Illinois, Michigan, and Massachusetts stood in stark contrast to the fiercely repressive atmosphere in the South, whose electoral power was also used to prevent liberal federal legislation being passed. All of this made it especially hard to produce coordinated responses across the territory of the union as a whole, particularly as industrial conditions could vary geographically so very much. It was then — and is now — very difficult to mobilize a society made up of so many almost independent states.

A final facet of diversity must be taken into account. Even at the height of the classic period of heavy industry, manual workers never formed anything like a majority of the labor force. Fundamental political change depended upon the making of cross-class alliances, which proved to be very hard to accomplish. Had the attempt of the populist movement to join workers with independent small farmers been successful, the United States might have moved in a Scandinavian direction, for it was precisely peasant-worker alliances there that formed the background for social democracy.[16] But that alliance failed in the United States, with all the factors mentioned so far playing negative roles: Catholics in the North felt threatened by the tones of Protestant revivalism so evident in William Jen-

---

[15] P. Davis, *Hometown: A Portrait of an American Community* (New York: Simon and Shuster, 1982), 200.

[16] G. Esping-Anderson, *Politics against Markets: The Social Democratic Route to Power* (Princeton, N.J.: Princeton University Press, 1985). It is worth noting that the most successful American movement in this direction — the Democratic Farmer Labor party — had its base in the predominantly Scandinavian areas of the Midwest.

nings Bryan's campaign of 1896, while racism in the South did much to discredit attempts to organize farmers, blacks, and workers in a common cause. A cross-class union was also thwarted by the undoubted fact that new immigrants, keen to make any sort of living, were easy to use as strikebreakers and formed the majority of unskilled laborers. Their foreignness, lack of skill, and reputation as scab workers, made it almost impossible to forge trade union alliances with them.[17]

The character of the working class can be thus be summarized as somewhat mixed, comprised at once of elements of genuine solidarity and of previous loyalties that cut across them. But the working class did not exist in isolation: to the contrary, it faced the very determined opposition of a powerful and entrenched capitalist class, whose actions ensured that socialist solidarity would never be able to overcome its own structural and institutional difficulties. The essential, unduly neglected fact of vital importance is the level of labor violence in American history. Between 1872 and 1914, seven, sixteen, and perhaps thirty-five workers died violently in Britain, Germany and France, respectively; in contrast, between five and eight *hundred* violent deaths of workers occurred in the United States.[18] The capitalist elite, riding a wave of self-confidence

---

[17] The same pattern continues to hold today, as new immigrants fill the least skilled roles, are segregated from elite workers, and are rarely unionized. For an example, see G. Genier et al., "On Machines and Bureaucracy: Controlling Ethnic Interaction in Miami's Apparel and Construction Industries," in L. Lamphere, ed., *Structuring Diversity: Ethnographic Perspectives on the New Immigration* (Chicago: University of Chicago Press, 1992).

[18] R. J. Goldstein, *Political Repression in Modern America* (Cambridge: Cambridge University Press, 1978), and *Political Repression in Nineteenth Century Europe* (London: Crook Helm, 1983), cited in Mann, *Sources of Social Power*, vol. 2, chap. 18. Of course, we must also take into account the generally higher level of violence in the United States, which is at

resulting from its massive corporate concentrations, and backed by a government that believed in the constitutional right to unlimited capital accumulation, was quite willing to call in the Pinkertons and sometimes troops (more often from states than from the federal government) to smash the strikes. In one of the most famous such instances, Carnegie and Frick deliberately sought to destroy the steelworkers in 1892 through the use of force and strikebreakers. Though Frick was stabbed, they were completely successful: Carnegie declared that life was again worth living, and Rockefeller sent congratulations.[19] This is one point at which the early institutional pattern of the country came to matter a very great deal. The capitalist offensive worked through the courts, as sympathetic judges declared union activity to be an illegal restraint on trade.[20] The fact that property rights had been encoded in the Constitution did much to ease the travails of the rich and powerful.

Because it was often blatantly linked to state power, the brutal capitalist counteroffensive might eventually have led to increased worker solidarity. But an important section of the working class responded in such a way as to rule this out. The key figure here is Samuel Gompers, the founder and long-serving first president of the American Federation of Labor (AFL), whose policies repudiated socialism in favor of creating a respectable "business union." Gompers saw clearly that socialism had little chance of success in the American climate and he insisted that capitalism created a distinct division of

---

least partly a reflection of the ethic of self-help. As we noted above, the unions also were relatively violent.

[19] H. Brogan, *The Pelican History of the United States* (London: Penguin, 1986), 432.

[20] S. Skowronek, *Building a New American State: The Expansion of National Administrative Capacities, 1877–1920* (Cambridge: Cambridge University Press, 1982).

interest between capital and labor. This allowed him to re-place the woolly idealism of the Knights with practical organizational skills: where the former started strikes and lost them through lack of union funds, Gompers pressured quietly but more effectively. He also offered something valuable to businesspeople, namely, the ability to have contractual agreements upheld, and they responded by recognizing his union. But if the AFL achieved much, it did so principally for the skilled, many of whom eventually moved out of the inner city to the suburbs — which encouraged them to think of themselves as something other than working class. A key element as well was union revenge on the immigrants who had for so long provided bosses with cheap labor. The greatest political success for the unions in this period was the Chinese Exclusion Act of 1882. Fear of competition from impoverished blacks was also part of the union movement; it was to play an ugly part in fueling working-class racism.[21]

The pattern of American labor relations was set by about 1900. There were, of course, further challenges, but they proved to be too little and too late. Votes for the Socialist party before 1914 helped the passing of the Clayton Act of 1914, but the act still allowed the courts to be used against conspiracies, for all its formal assertion of labor's rights. The National Labor Relations Act of 1935 did finally grant unions collective bargaining, furthering the cause of industrial unionism. But the rise of the Congress of Industrial Organizations (CIO) did not undermine the AFL, so sectionalism continued to blunt the force of labor. Recent interpretations of the New Deal legislation on unions even suggest that apparent union gains were actually counterbalanced by greater state regulation.[22] This is

[21] G. W. Fredrickson, *White Supremacy* (Oxford: Oxford University Press, 1981).

[22] C. L. Tomlins, *The State and the Unions: Labor Relations, Law, and the*

to stress that the New Deal did more to save than to challenge American capitalism. As this view is heresy in some quarters, a final point should be made. The increase in state presence and in union membership ascribable to the New Deal has proved to be an episode, an interruption to a more basic American pattern. When recent changes in the occupational structure are also brought to mind it becomes quite apparent that no further class challenge from below can be expected.

A final source of the relative passivity of American workers should be noted, namely, the absorption of workers into a culture of consumption, which has followed from suburbanization and increased wealth, at least amongst the skilled. This process began when the great urban department stores of the nineteenth century offered the public vast arrays of goods in a palatial atmosphere. Instead of intimate shops catering to a knowledgeable elite, these new environments offered huge spaces that anyone could enter, regardless of class background. This turned shopping into a communal and democratic act: "The consumer now was being persuaded not merely to become a customer but to join a consumption community. He was being offered something that was not just for him but for everybody like him."[23] In its present-day incarnation, the consumption community is reproduced in the protected, artificial, hygienic, and homogenizing environment of the mall. Freely strolling through the various consumption universes offered by a myriad of specialty stores, customers can peruse, comment upon, and purchase the status symbols that indicate their relative wealth, while also confirming their individuality by choosing the goods

---

Organized Labor Movement in America, 1880–1960 (Cambridge: Cambridge University Press, 1985).

[23] D. Boorstin, "Consumer's Palaces," in R. Boorstin, ed., *The Daniel J. Boorstin Reader* (New York: Modern Library, 1995), 253.

that signify a life style.[24] There are class divisions here: some malls and the goods they offer are for the relatively wealthy; others are for the relatively poor. Still, in all of them, the carefully controlled environment and the overwhelming display of items for sale is a tangible representation of a communal fantasy of achieving and displaying material wealth; furthermore, "having chosen to purchase the same item creates an immediate affinity among Americans if they meet."[25] Hoping for success themselves, very few Americans have any desire to overthrow an enormously productive marketplace, which has filled palaces of consumption with the dreams that money can buy.

[24] J. Jacobs, *The Mall: An Attempted Escape from Everyday Life* (Prospect Heights, N.J.: Waveland Press, 1984), offers a symbolic analysis of the place of the mall within American culture.

[25] W. O Beeman, "Freedom to Choose: Symbols and Values in American Advertising," in H. Varenne, ed., *Symbolizing America* (Lincoln: University of Nebraska Press, 1986), 59.

The world in America, America in the world

The United States differs from Europe in having had to bear a minimal military burden for most of its recorded history.[1] Even the initial move toward world power, at the turn of the century, did not lead the United States to anything like a European norm of military expenditure. Military disbursements rose only with participation in two world wars. In both instances, participation was, so to speak, well timed in that entry was late enough to avoid exhausting both economy and society. Against this, however, must be set the continuing military burden America has had to carry after 1945, due to expensive conflicts in Korea and in Vietnam, and to the cold war effort to contain Communism. For fifty years, America has had a larger defense budget than that of any of its allies. The central claim of this section follows from this: the most important social dynamic in twentieth-century American history has been its increased involvement in the world.

Analysis in this area must concentrate on the two issues hinted at in the chapter's title, taking each in turn even while noting the complex interaction between them. First, participation in war can have huge consequences for domestic political arrangements. We have seen the close correlation between military participation and democracy in the early years of the American republic. That conscription warfare in twentieth-century Europe led to the creation and extension of a whole

---

[1] Measuring the military burden involves many technical problems; for an attempt to deal with most such difficulties for the period 1870–1914, see J. A. Hall, *Coercion and Consent: Studies on the Modern State* (Cambridge: Polity Press, 1994), chap. 8. Note that some of the continuing burden resulting from the Civil War (when American expenditures *were* high), namely, military pensions, is counted in civilian expenditure, as was often the case with other countries. For an account of such pensions, see T. Skocpol, *Protecting Soldiers and Mothers: The Political Origins of Social Policy in the United States* (Cambridge: Harvard University Press, 1992).

series of social benefits is generally appreciated.[2] The rise and fall of the American civil rights movement can likewise be understood only once account is taken of foreign policy involvement. The second issue is that of security. A fundamental cause of social dissolution of great states throughout history has been the fatigue brought on by continual struggle with rival powers. Those who assert that industrial capitalism needs a leader who can ensure that markets remain open also worry that the strains of leadership may be so great as eventually to lead to economic decline. This contention fueled the last great debate about the future of America, which took place around Paul Kennedy's claim that the United States was likely to decline as had Great Britain.[3] This view never made much sense; the benefit of hindsight allows us firmly to reject it. America's position in the world is preeminent, while its economy has enduring strengths.

It may be as well to retreat a little from some of the generalizations already made. In particular, there is a sense in which the United States has always been interested in life outside its immediate borders. Killing American Indians, acquiring Louisiana and Texas, war with Mexico, and the doctrine of Manifest Destiny all show the depth of American external involvement from the very beginning of the republic. Further, a fundamental change did occur in the early twentieth century: a division of geopolitical labor had begun to take place between the United States and Great Britain, leaving the former to balance Japan and the latter free to concentrate on the threat from Germany.[4] Nonetheless, American domestic ar-

---

[2] A. Marwick, *War and Social Change in the Twentieth Century* (London: Macmillan, 1974).

[3] P. Kennedy, *The Rise and Decline of the Great Powers* (New York: Random House, 1987).

[4] A. Offer, *The First World War: An Agrarian Interpretation* (Oxford: Oxford

rangements were not as yet much affected by the world. On the one hand, the demand for involvement in world affairs had a narrow domestic base, in large part supplied by conservative members of the eastern establishment eager to integrate new immigrants in an American cause. On the other hand, war with Spain led to such ferocious anti-war feeling that America turned its back on large-scale territorial annexation.[5]

Involvement in world wars was an altogether more consequential matter. The emergence of the Soviet Union led to "Red scares" at the end of both world wars.[6] Less obvious but of huge importance was the effect of war upon the economy. The South benefited from wartime expansion, and at last became integrated into a genuinely national economy. In addition, military production during the Second World War did what the New Deal had not been able to achieve: it restored the economy to health. This in turn led to the growth of the federal government, giving it for the first time genuine power over the states. Most important, the temporary ending of immigration combined with labor shortages in the industrial sector in such a way as to advantage African Americans. These were the years of the Great Migration of blacks to the North. This is not to say that change was easy or automatic. The experience

---

University Press, 1989); H. B. Ryan, *The Vision of Anglo-America* (Cambridge: Cambridge University Press, 1987).

[5] W. Widenor, *Henry Cabot Lodge and the Search for an American Foreign Policy* (Berkeley: University of California Press, 1980); H. K. Beale, *Theodore Roosevelt and the Rise of America to World Power* (New York: Collier, 1967); R. L. Beisner, *Twelve against Empire* (Chicago: University of Chicago Press, 1985).

[6] The first emergence of the idea of "multiculturalism" took place against a panicky background of near-forcible assimilation of German-Americans. For details of the views of Horace Kallen and Randolph Bourne, see M. Lind, *The Next American Nation: The New Nationalism and the Fourth American Revolution* (New York: Free Press, 1995), chap. 2.

of the First World War was made especially unhappy by large and vicious riots of whites against blacks in northern cities and by the spurning of black veterans. But this did not stop black Americans from later volunteering in great numbers to fight against Hitler's racism. The impact of war upon African Americans, especially those from the urban centers of the North, can scarcely be exaggerated. Many black soldiers were forcibly reminded of the prejudices rampant in their own country by the segregation of the armed forces — made the more striking when German prisoners of war received treatment that was denied to American blacks. One black Alabama corporal noted in 1945:

> I spent four years in the Army to free a bunch of Dutchmen and Frenchmen, and I'm hanged if I'm going to let the Alabama version of the Germans kick me around when I get home. No sirree-bob! I went into the Army a nigger; I'm comin' out a *man*.[7]

This sort of determination in conjunction with improved economic life chances meant that a serious challenge to the central injustice of American life was sure to be mounted.

It is no accident that the civil rights movement functioned most powerfully in the South. Segregation solidified social institutions, notably the Baptist Church, which offered a staging ground for mass movements led by a middle-class black leadership whose fate was bound up with their fellows because they had no possibility of exit. Furthermore, the racism of the state gave the movement a clear target. This allowed a many-pronged crusade of enormous courage and high spiritual force to mount challenges to the varied practices of segregation in

---

[7] J. C. Goulden, *The Best Years, 1945–1950* (New York: Atheneum, 1976), 353, cited in J. Patterson, *Grand Expectations: The United States, 1945–1974* (Oxford: Oxford University Press, 1996), 23.

the South. If the tactics of boycotts, sit-ins, and freedom rides were imaginative, the larger nonviolent strategy was brilliant — especially in contrast to the flagrant brutality of such figures of repression as Eugene ("Bull") Connor, the public safety commissioner of Montgomery, Alabama. It was above all Dr. Martin Luther King, Jr., who, by stressing the need to appeal to the divided conscience of Americans in the North through moral protest, ensured that federal power would be used in a second reconstruction.[8] One enabling factor that helped here was television, for this was the first social movement that was viewed in the living rooms of most Americans.

But still more important was the effect of a change in elite attitudes *caused by involvement with the world.* In the face of Soviet propaganda, the political elite realized that if America were to lead the democratic world, the scandal of racial injustice had to be confronted. This played its part in Truman's decision to desegregate the armed forces. Moral authority in the world mattered even more to both Eisenhower and Kennedy. Both sent troops once again into the South; this time, the huge increase in federal power meant that local white resistance did not have to be accommodated.[9]

Reform was not achieved smoothly. Kennedy's legislation became bogged down in Congress, partly because he was well aware that dangers for the Democratic party lay in pushing ahead too fast. Accordingly, an element of real importance was Lyndon Johnson's formidable political skill, brought to bear as he sought to show himself a worthy heir to the Kennedy legacy. His presidency did more for African Americans, first in

---

[8] D. J. Garrow, *Bearing the Cross: Martin Luther King, Jr., and the Southern Christian Leadership Conference* (New York: Vintage Books, 1986).

[9] A. Marx, *Making Race and Nation: A Comparison of the United States, South Africa, and Brazil* (Cambridge: Cambridge University Press, 1998), chap. 9.

ending segregation and ensuring the right to vote and then in legislation against poverty, than any other in American history after Lincoln. This is not to say that Johnson was a model of perfection: to the contrary, he felt that little was needed beyond voting rights, and became irritated with black leaders who demanded more — especially since he was sensible that the Democrats had lost key states in the South in the midst of his electoral triumph in 1964. Further, the legislation against poverty was so poorly funded as to amount to a skirmish rather than a war. Nonetheless, the achievements were real and significant: formal segregation was more or less destroyed, poverty reduced, the initial rise of a substantial black middle class solidified, and racism itself somewhat abated — in large measure because of the powerful charismatic moral force provided by King himself.

Segregation was such a flagrant and open breach of American ideals as to make intervention sooner or later inevitable. The removal of de jure segregation has therefore enhanced the stability of American politics. This is *not*, even for a moment, to say that the oldest and greatest problem of American life has been completely resolved through the final triumph of a new reconstruction establishing generalized justice. The ways in which this problem continues to plague America concern us below; our immediate task is analysis of the destruction of the political coalition that made desegregation possible in the first place. The disturbing sociological point that has to be made is that the depoliticization and fragmentation of the movement enhanced political stability in America. This point should not be misunderstood. For one thing, this route to stability was morally repulsive. For another, stability would have been more fully assured — that is, without the continuing possibility of rage-filled outbursts of riot — had the different route of more complete implementation of racial justice been followed. There are several reasons why this was not to be so.

As King found out in the course of his rather unsuccessful 1966 campaign in Chicago, it proved to be much harder to mobilize against economic inequality than it had been to tackle Jim Crow. The fight for desegregation had been solidified and intensified by the southern states' sponsorship of racial exclusion; the struggle for economic justice presented no equally clear target against which to mobilize — which in turn meant that there were fewer historical black organizations available as resources for mobilization. Success in achieving civil rights thus paradoxically undermined African American solidarity in the long run. At a theoretical level, this is the converse of our argument that escalation of conflict results from the layering of different points of contention on top of one another. Here, we see that when such layering ceases to be visible, unity suffers. Reconstructionist efforts were also stymied by white backlash. Fundamental change is always painful, but attempts to expand the efforts of reconstruction were damaged by the wider political turbulence of the 1960s. Raised expectations in the African American community were exacerbated by the general malaise of the Vietnam War era and by the continued poverty and marginalization of the ghettos; the whole vicious stew was brought to the boil by political assassinations that produced violent inner-city riots. While this led occasionally to the passing of legislation by crisis, the diminution of King's moral legacy undermined much needed support outside the African American community.

These were the sorts of circumstances in which Richard Nixon's politics of resentment could flourish. While it is true that Nixon's earliest years in office had liberal domestic elements attached, the deeper structure of his period in power showed an altogether meaner agenda at work — an expression both of his personality and of his need to counter the threat of George Wallace, whose racist southern populism enjoyed sudden electoral support. Nixon himself did everything he could to slow down desegregation in schooling, especially by clear opposition to busing. Much of this was part of his "southern strategy," designed to pick up the votes lost by Johnson's civil rights initiatives. But the talk of a neglected, patriotic "Silent Majority"—whose fears were so played up, at Nixon's behest, by Vice President Agnew—was also designed to turn the white working class against reform. The insistence that special privileges were being given to African Americans did much to create the white ethnic reaction that debilitated the War on Poverty.[10] Republican leaders after Nixon went the same route: Reagan attacked "welfare mothers," while Bush's infamous Willie Horton campaign advertisements played equally shamelessly on white fear of blacks.

The tactics involved in this strategy can be highlighted by turning to Tocqueville's final and most sophisticated reflection on distrust in social life. The intellectual question that animates his greatest work, *The Old Regime and the French Revolution,* is why the French people were unable to cooperate to run their affairs in liberty after they had disposed of the king. Analyzing the sorry state of his own society, Tocqueville abandoned his early, jejune belief that democracy in and of itself would lead to envious distrust unless countered by popular involvement in local level community organizations. He saw instead that the seeds of discord were spread and a paralyzed culture of conflict created from above, by a politically astute elite who consciously fomented rancor and divisiveness among groups so as the better to rule over all of them.[11] Similar divide-and-rule tactics worked well for Nixon, too, leaving social dis-

---

[10] J. Quadagno, *The Color of Welfare* (New York: Oxford University Press, 1998); Patterson, *Grand Expectations,* chap. 23.

[11] A. de Tocqueville, *The Old Regime and the French Revolution* (reprint, New York: Anchor Books, 1969), 136.

trust as his abiding legacy; he made ethnic politics popular, although this label is but a mask for the real division he left behind — that of the many against the few.

Another factor to which attention must be given is the increasing splits within the African American community. A wholly comprehensible divergence over political strategy — at times, as with W.E.B. Du Bois, present within a single individual — has often characterized African American politics. On one side, stand those who wish to pressure white America into allowing assimilation and equity; on the other hand are more disgruntled activists, often driven to embrace separatism. The split that had occurred between Malcolm X and Martin Luther King, Jr., is representative of this internal division — although their rift might possibly have been healed had both not been killed. There is no doubt, however, that lack of unity thereafter — at times consciously fostered by Republicans seeking to court black intellectuals — has weakened the African American community.[12]

At least as important is a social split, which again has connections to the victory in the struggle for civil rights. That victory allowed middle-class African Americans to move out of urban ghettos in search of a better life in the suburbs — which, ironically, quickly became segregated by "white flight." This move deprived those left behind of experienced organizers and recognized political leaders. The city cores were also left without a skilled work force, while economic shifts to the periphery simultaneously emptied the cities of the blue-collar manual labor jobs that working-class ghetto dwellers had traditionally held.[13] To some degree, poverty was alleviated by the burgeoning drug trade, as the inner city became the supermarket

---

[12] Marx, *Making Race and Nation*, chap. 9.

[13] W. J. Wilson, *When Work Disappears: The World of the New Urban Poor* (New York: Knopf, 1996).

where middle-class consumers could purchase illegal thrills. Unhappily, the upward mobility that drug money permitted was more than offset by the terrible social and psychological devastation caused in the inner city by addiction and turf warfare.[14] In sum, the advances made by civil rights legislation permitted the rise of a new, upwardly mobile black suburban middle class at the cost of the ruin of the remaining residents of the ghetto.

A final troubled speculation on the question of race returns us to the question of foreign involvement. At present, military costs are a diminishing burden on the economy. America looks particularly secure internationally and does not appear to have any need for large-scale involvement overseas. The future may bring "spectator sport" wars, such as those in Panama and in Grenada, but large-scale, long-lasting infantry warfare seems unlikely. The fact that fewer American deaths are likely to occur abroad in the next years is certainly something to celebrate. But the absence of conscription and the development of a purely professional army make pressures for democratization and inclusion less likely, while decreases in the size of the armed forces may limit what has become an extremely important avenue of social mobility for African Americans. There may not be another Colin Powell. All of this is said tentatively, as must be the case given the lack of predictability of international affairs — to whose general contours it is now time to turn.

American postwar foreign policy has been enormously successful. The growing flood of documents released in Moscow is making it clearer than ever that the Soviet Union posed a genuine geopolitical threat, whose containment was a great

---

[14] For a chilling example, see Philippe Bourgois, *In Search of Respect: Selling Crack in El Barrio* (Cambridge: Cambridge University Press, 1995).

historical achievement.[15] The success of this policy rested on two domestic pillars. On the one hand, an exceptionally unified American elite, aware of the disasters that followed the isolationism of the interwar period, jumped at the chance of ruling the world, and took good care to ensure that British power was sufficiently diminished to make this possible.[16] On the other hand, popular anti-Communism helped draw warweary Americans into foreign involvement by giving intervention the character of a moral crusade, an approach finally cemented by the Korean War. But equal in importance to the containment of the Soviet Union was reconstruction within capitalist society. Willing partners in Japan and Europe, whose leaders actively sought an American presence, both to provide security and to help remove the extreme elements of left and right that had plagued their own political systems, helped create an "empire by invitation."[17] Japan and Germany became trading states, while a network of international institutions ensured the hegemony of free trade.[18]

It seemed at one time that the war in Vietnam had destroyed all of this. Because the government was both unwilling and unable to raise taxes, the cost of the war in combination with the Great Society program created a deficit so sizable that the dollar was forced off gold, with America thereby seeming

[15] J. L. Gaddis, *We Now Know: Rethinking Cold War History* (Oxford: Oxford University Press, 1997).

[16] W. Isaacson and E. Thomas, *The Wise Men* (New York: Simon and Schuster, 1986), offers an account of the elite; for the policy toward Britain, see R. Gardner, *Sterling-Dollar Diplomacy* (London: Macmillan, 1969).

[17] G. Lundestad, "Empire by Invitation?" *Journal of Peace Research* 23 (1986): 263–77.

[18] R. Keohane, *After Hegemony* (Princeton, N.J.: Princton Univesity Press, 1984).

to lose the "seigniorage" rights that come to the manager of a top currency. Still more seriously, a split seemed to be surfacing in the political elite, as conservatives argued that the prospect of electoral retribution made it impossible to retreat from Vietnam. Yet anti-war protestors were right to say that Vietnam was not truly vital to America's national interest.[19] Congress responded to popular pressure with a review of foreign policy, which resulted in eventual retirement from the conflict. The way in which democratic examination of involvement in Vietnam encouraged withdrawal is accordingly a sign of strength rather than of weakness in the way in which foreign affairs are managed within the United States.[20] To make these points is, of course, to assert what should now be obvious, namely, that the "loss" of Vietnam has not in fact destroyed America's place in the world. Crucially, there have been no more Vietnams: the lesson of overextension was learnt and the unity of the elite maintained, freeing the United States to concentrate on matters genuinely vital to its national interest.

With these background comments in mind, let us confront directly the question of decline. The argument that America must pay a dire price for its international leadership seems to be wrong. There was never much similarity between the situation that confronted Britain in the 1890s and the one that has

---

[19] For a history of American anti-war movements, see S. Tax, "War and the Draft," in M. Fried, M. Harris, and R. Murphy, eds., *War* (Garden City, N.Y.: Doubleday, 1968).

[20] We therefore do not fully accept Tocqueville's view, as endorsed by Kennan in relation to general theory and by Kissinger in relation to Vietnam, that democracy is fundamentally antithetical to the rational conduct of foreign policy. A de Toqueville, *Democracy in America* (reprint, New York: Anchor Books, 1969) 645–51; G. Kennan, *American Diplomacy* (Chicago: University of Chicago Press, 1951); H. A. Kissinger, *White House Years* (Boston: Little, Brown, 1982).

faced America since 1971.[21] For one thing, there was no equivalent of Imperial Germany facing the United States: America's major geopolitical rival was the Soviet Union, which stood outside capitalist society, while its economic rivals within capitalism were geopolitically dependent upon it. American power was so great that it enjoyed privileges, notably that of having its deficit financed by its allies, to whom it exported its inflation. Our central point is simply that changes in recent years have enhanced and not diminished the international standing of the United States.

The collapse of the Soviet Union, together with the undoubted American domination of the new revolution in military technology, means that the United States stands supreme in military and geopolitical terms. Some of America's often needless and mistaken intervention in third world countries was the result of competition with a genuine geopolitical rival, whose demise means that relative withdrawal will not adversely affect security. In these circumstances, the military burden is decreasing — without danger, it should be noted, given American technological leadership. The modern plague of terrorism is an admission of the incapacity of opponents to mount any frontal assault on American power.

The economic and financial hegemony of America shows its continued strength, as mention of even a few indicators demonstrates. The loss of the preeminence naturally caused by the recovery of debilitated economies bottomed out in the early 1970s, with the United States thereafter holding more or less the same share as it had previously.[22] It seems further that

---

[21] For a detailed defense of this claim, see Hall, *Coercion and Consent*, chap. 7.

[22] J. Nye, *Bound to Lead* (New York: Basic Books, 1990). Cf. S. Strange, "The Persistent Myth of Lost Hegemony," *International Organization* 41 (1987): 551–74.

America is regaining competitive edge in middle-sized com-
panies;[23] the most recent study suggests that the United States
continues to dominate the newest areas of high-technology
goods.[24] Finally, the capital of the world — which still banks in
the dollar — flew to the United States in the 1980s, largely as
the result of Reaganomics. This capital flow was at the expense
of developing societies, and it makes the third world's attempt
to control its minerals and commodities pale into insignifi-
cance.[25] All these factors should, of course, be set in the context of the situation facing others: the structural problems of
Japan will not be resolved for many years, while Europe looks
set for difficulty in the future because countries within the European Union that retain their own currencies will be able to
improve their competitive status by means of devaluation. The
summary conclusion to all of this is obvious and straightforward: as the world's leading power, America has the capacity —
uniquely so in an increasingly interdependent world — of deciding its own fate, relatively free of intervention from abroad.

[23] "A Portrait of America's New Competitiveness," *The Economist*, June 4,
1988, 57–58.

[24] R. McCulloch, *The Challenge to U.S. Leadership in High Technology Industries* (Cambridge, Mass.: National Bureau of Economic Research,
1988). Cf. "Back on Top?" *The Economist*, September 16, 1995.

[25] S. Krasner, *Structural Conflict* (Berkeley: University of California Press,
1984).

Reprise

Four dangerous crises in American history have been identified, the argument being that overcoming these has led to an increase in political stability. These crises can be reviewed, before accentuating the general argument by considering mechanisms of stability and by noting the obvious comparison to the collapse of the Soveit Union.

The first moment of genuine division was at the very end of the eighteenth century, when it seemed that Federalists favoring the increased power of the state were prepared to act with force against their political opponents. This raised the prospect that the Jeffersonians, aided by a still radical populace, might reply in kind, and so occasion civil war. In fact, power was peacefully transferred, with the Jeffersonians thereafter not just refusing to embark on any strategy of revenge but in fact carrying out the political program of the Federalists to boot. Further, a background consensus was slowly created to regulate conflict by means of a stable and flexible dual party system; from that point on, the institutionalization of a loyal opposition did much to diminish the intensity of internal political conflict. But this newfound unity was made fragile by the regional distinctiveness of the South, and the whole national fabric shattered as abolitionist fervor and uneven economic development led to the Civil War. As we have seen, the end result was a greatly solidified and homogenized nation, although black Americans remained excluded from the mainstream. The third moment, that of the emergence of collectivist socialist ideas, had a rather different resolution. Radicalism from below failed to triumph because of the intersection of a number of factors: American individualism and social mobility pressed against union solidarity, as did internal divisions and cross-cutting political alliances, while of equal importance was repression by a capitalist elite making full use of court interpretations of the Constitution. Finally, American entrance onto the international stage increased the anger and the economic capabilities of African Americans, while making the political elite, conscious of its place in the world, receptive to a new reconstruction. The political successes of the civil rights movement increased stability in a paradoxical fashion: political inclusion represented justice, but it depoliticized America's historic sore — which remains but partially healed. Meanwhile, American world power has not led to economic or political decline. All in all, the United States appears more stable and secure than ever before, internationally and nationally.

The stability that has come to characterize American politics rests on a set of factors implicit in this account. First, the defeat of genuine societal alternatives has meant that American politics operates within a very narrow range: there is no sign that national unity is likely to be challenged anew, and every indication that a unified establishment exists, prepared to defend its interests if need be. Second, political citizenship, formerly the preserve of white males but now accessible at last not just to women but to other races as well, has diffused conflicts throughout society, in part by means of the party system — making it very difficult indeed for the society to concentrate on a single set of issues for any extended period of time. Meanwhile, the state has refrained from intervention in major areas of social life, allowing these to proceed within civil society according to their own logic; this means there has been little of the politicization of social movements and intensification of conflict that results when state actions are layered on top of other social divisions. Third, America has, of course, benefited from economic abundance, enabling the country to paper over cracks of principle by means of the pleasures derived from economic growth. Finally, we have stressed a negative: the lack of any geopolitical rival able to knock America off its perch as the hegemonic leader of capitalist society has allowed it to continue to enjoy the privileges of seigniorage.

These general points about American stability can be under-scored by means of a comparison. It is hard to recall that a mere twenty-five years or so ago, voices were raised in the academy suggesting that democracy was coming apart at the seams, most obviously because rising demands could only be met by means of inflationary policies sure to undermine the prosperity of the economy.[1] Virtually everything about this view has been proved wrong, notably the assumption that in-flation was caused by pressure from below and the belief that democracies could not tame it.[2] But what is most striking is that these theorists assumed that America was essentially un-governable. The contrast was with the authoritarian structure of command in the Soviet Union and its satraps, which, it was thought, lent those societies a great comparative advantage.

Of course, we now know that the Soviet political economy as a whole always faced the instability that comes with rigidity. To establish an independent trade union or even to hold a strike meant a battle against the state. If the impact of Soli-darity on the whole socialist system should not be forgotten, the eventual collapse of the Soviet Union owed most to other, interrelated factors. The first was that the cold war imposed a burden of military expenditure on the Soviet empire that was genuinely debilitating; this particularly mattered given the in-efficacy of central planning as a means of managing late indus-trial economic affairs. The absence of civil society, which had been attacked by the tsars and destroyed by the Bolsheviks,

---

[1] The most striking statement of a very general view was M. Crozier, S. Huntington, and J. Watanuki, *The Crisis of Democracy* (New York: New York University Press, 1975).

[2] M. Smith, *Power, Norms and Inflation* (New York: Aldine de Gruyter, 1992). Cf. J. A. Hall, *Coercion and Consent: Studies on the Modern State* (Cambridge: Polity Press, 1994), chap. 2.

made it impossible for a reforming leader to find partners with whom to engage in a process of controlled liberalization.[3] The power vacuum that resulted gave ethnic nationalities their chance to step in and destroy the system completely. All this illuminates the social flexibility, cohesiveness, and economic success of the United States by sheer contrast. Clearly, the stability of America is not in question, however extensive the social ills are with which it has to deal.

[3] R. Bova, "Political Dynamics of the Post-communist Transition: A Comparative Perspective," *World Politics* 44 (1991): 113–38; J. A. Hall, "A View of a Death: On Communism, Ancient and Modern," *Theory and Society* 27 (1998): 509–34.

Sociability in America

PART TWO

T H E charge that Americans are so individualist as to have nothing in common has been made again and again. We have seen that Tocqueville introduced this theme, and that it has reappeared even more forcefully in the recent flood of worried accounts of American society. Contemporary philosophers have added further bite to this charge by claiming that "malaise" or "discontent" results from the "unencumbered" Robinson Crusoe–like self held to be typical of Americans.[1] A characteristically ugly portrait of the supposed misery of the isolated individualist is offered by Michael Walzer:

> I imagine a human being thoroughly divorced, freed of parents, spouse and children, watching pornographic performances in some dark theater, joining (it may be his only membership) this or that odd cult, which he will probably leave in a month or two for another still odder. Is this a liberated human being?[2]

It is a small step from accepting this picture to arguing, as did Tocqueville, that the moral weakness of the solipsistic individual might very possibly lead to a mindless conformity and voluntary enslavement to an all-powerful state.[3]

---

[1] C. Taylor, *The Malaise of Modernity* (Concord, Ont.: Anansi, 1991); M. Sandel, *Liberalism and the Limits of Justice* (Cambridge: Cambridge University Press, 1982), and *Democracy's Discontent* (Cambridge: Harvard University Press, 1996).

[2] M. Walzer, *Radical Principles* (New York: Basic Books, 1980), 6.

[3] "[When] no man is obliged to put his powers at the disposal of another, and no one has any claim of right to substantial support from his fellow man, each is both independent and weak . . . his weakness makes him feel the need for some outside help which he cannot expect from any of his fellows, for they are both impotent and cold. In this extremity he naturally turns his eyes toward that huge entity which alone stands out above the universal level of abasement. His needs, and even more his longings,

If America is indeed nothing but such a set of unconnected individuals, then the structural framework we have described would probably not be enough to offset Tocqueville's qualms. This point applies to another claim, that Americans have no need of a common cultural identity because they are protected from moral anarchy by a shared reverence for the Constitution.[4] We need to keep in mind, however, that ideals cannot be institutionally imposed, but must resonate with preexistent shared perceptions and ways of being in the world. Many societies, after all, have wonderfully democratic and liberal constitutions, yet manage to be totalitarian and genocidal despite them. Furthermore, grade-school civics lessons aside, very few Americans have any clear idea of what the Constitution or the Bill of Rights contains, yet they are Americans all the same, instantly recognizable not by their differences but by their enormous similarities.

Our argument follows Max Weber's suggestion that America is not and has never been a "sand pile." We spend most of our time outlining the contents of the culture, beginning with its conceptual apparatus and sacred values

---

continually put him in mind of that entity, and he ends by regarding it as the sole and necessary support of his individual weakness." A. de Tocqueville, *Democracy in America* (reprint, New York: Anchor Books, 1969), 672.

[4] M. Walzer, "What Does It Mean to Be an American?" *Social Research* 57 (1990): 591–614, suggests that it is sufficient for "hyphenated Americans" to rest their political faith in the American side of the hyphen, leaving their cultural identity in the left. Oddly, the leftist communitarian Walzer finds himself here allied with the more conservative Samuel Huntington, who insists that "if it were not for the American creed, what would Americans have in common?" S. Huntington, *American Politics: The Promise of Disharmony* (Cambridge: Harvard University Press, 1981), 24. Huntington's position is in fact more nuanced than Walzer's. He stresses the quasi-mystical and ambiguous aspects of American creedal beliefs in a manner that is compatible with the argument we will make.

before turning to anxieties shown toward politics and associational life. Quite as important as the demonstration of sociability within the cultural code, however, is the analytically separate claim, central to the last few chapters, that most Americans participate within and share the values of this particular way of life.

This last assertion means that we are skeptical of the argument that generalizations about American life necessarily neglect the voices of the oppressed or excluded.[5] The analysis offered in Part One did not discount acts of repression in the maintenance of American culture: to the contrary, violence played a decisive role in crushing native societies, southern ideology, and the socialist option. Further, struggle has long marked definitions of the boundaries of the cultural code: Catholics had to counter Protestant dominance, while Italians and Irish once had to combat being stigmatized as racially inferior. Nonetheless, it is a fact that America has become remarkably homogeneous, and that truly distinctive beliefs have been sanitized so as to fit into American ideals: celebration of Hinduism, for example, is excellent just so long as its central component, stratification by caste, is ignored. If ethnicity is becoming an option, an area of choice, we are well aware that race remains a matter of destiny, an ascriptive status resulting from prejudice.[6] In other words, Americans do not *all* participate equally — a truth made especially cruel by the fact that most African Americans share the norms of the very culture which excludes them.

[5] R. Rosaldo, *Culture and Truth: The Remaking of Social Analysis* (Boston: Beacon Press, 1989); R. M. Smith, "Beyond Tocqueville, Myrdal and Hartz: The Multiple Traditions in America," *American Political Science Review* 87 (1993): 549–66.

[6] M. Waters, *Ethnic Options: Choosing Identities in America* (Berkeley: University of California Press, 1990).

Conceptual baselines

One of the most powerful founding arguments of sociology was made in the opening pages of Emile Durkheim's *The Elementary Forms of Religious Life*.[1] Immanuel Kant was wrong, Durkheim insisted, to suggest that our conceptual equipment comes from the structure of our minds; to the contrary, our notions of time, space, and causation are given to us by our society. In this section we will outline three American ways of grasping the world. The first is abstraction and vagueness in relation to political theory, the second is a pragmatic modular approach to reality, and the third is a faith that the self can be transformed. We concentrate on these factors rather than offering a complete account of the conceptual framework of the American worldview, because each is conducive to social homogeneity and antithetical to animosity and fragmentation.[2]

One thing that has often been held to characterize Americans is the ambiguity, confusion, and "contagious vagueness" of their understanding of political theory.[3] Americans may know, for example, that citizens have rights, but are extremely unclear about what those rights might be; they know Americans are supposed to be free, but not how freedom is limited, or what freedoms are permitted; they know that "all men are created equal," but cannot reconcile that precept with the protection of property.[4] In other words, most Americans are very proud indeed of the principles that their country is built upon,

---

[1] E. Durkheim, Introduction to *The Elementary Forms of Religious Life* (reprint, Glencoe, Ill.: Free Press, 1965).

[2] Tocqueville attempted such a complete picture in the second volume of *Democracy in America*.

[3] The term is from D. Boorstin, "The Mythologizing of George Washington," in R. Boorstin, ed., *The Daniel J. Boorstin Reader* (New York: Modern Library, 1995), 184.

[4] For some characteristic American confusions on these topics, see J. Hochschild, *What's Fair? American Beliefs about Distributive Justice* (Cambridge: Harvard University Press, 1981).

but for them those principles consist primarily of abstract notions, such as liberty, justice, and equality, rather than a systematic set of specific precepts or practices.

The major sources of "contagious vagueness" are to be discovered in the priority Americans have always given to pragmatic experience over philosophical system-building. Under the fluid circumstances of American life, ambivalence and woolly abstraction have certain advantages. "In a continually changing situation," Tocqueville noted, Americans "are never obliged by unchanging circumstances to stick firmly to any view once held. . . . they never know whether what they say today will fit the facts of tomorrow."[5] While remaining faithful to nebulous abstractions of "freedom," "individualism," and "equality," Americans can still be pliable in action without betraying their integrity or finding themselves immobilized by contradiction. Ideological vagueness thus allows Americans to feel a sense of unity without the trouble of actually considering exactly what that unity is based upon.

The abstraction and ambiguity of taken-for-granted foundational principles also allows Americans easily to "hold contradictory ideas simultaneously without bothering to resolve the potential conflict between them."[6] This, too, is not necessarily a bad thing in a pluralistic society, where central authority is relatively weak. The blurry quality of American assumptions about their shared creed allows them to accept innovations easily, so long as the innovations are metaphorically bathed in the aura of tradition, and to react according to circumstances without too much concern about agreement with prior positions. Most important, an ability to ignore contradiction permits

[5] A. de Tocqueville, *Democracy in America* (reprint, New York: Anchor Books, 1969), 482.

[6] R. McCloskey, "The American Ideology," in M. Irish, ed., *Continuing Crisis in American Politics* (Englewood Cliffs, N.J.: Prentice-Hall, 1963, 14.

Americans to overlook disputes that might tear a more ideologically consistent society apart.

Corresponding to American abstraction and vagueness in the realm of political philosophy is a positive can-do approach to life's ordinary problems. Practical hands-on "commonsense," it is believed, is capable of overcoming almost any obstacle, while "thinking too much" leads to nothing but confusion. It is no surprise that the predominant American philosophy is pragmatism, which decisively eschews theory under the assumption that coherent and consistent premises do not really matter much for achieving serviceable results.[7] However, what pragmatism takes for granted as "common sense" is actually a culturally constructed perspective, based in large measure on what has recently been called modular thinking. This is a strategy for instrumental action which assumes that complex wholes can be broken into elementary parts; these parts can then be efficiently recombined according to need. Modular thinking is American to the core: it is an atomistic, flexible, anti-organic, and anti-authoritarian view of the world — one which dispenses with tradition in favor of efficiency, and places all alternatives on an equal footing, subject to personal evaluation by the active innovator, who decides which combination is best.[8]

---

[7] Richard Rorty is the latest and most brilliant exemplar of a tradition that includes William James, John Dewey, and Wilard Van Orman Quine. Note, too, that the social contract theory of John Rawls's celebrated *A Theory of Justice* (Cambridge: Harvard University Press, 1971) is similarly culture bound, positing as its premise a world inhabited by discussion-prone academics. Of course, the major problem for pragmatists is a complete incapacity to defend any grounds (except so-called common sense) for deciding what is and is not beneficial. On this, see E. Gellner's essays on Quine in his *Spectacles and Predicaments* (Cambridge: Cambridge University Press, 1978).

[8] B. Shore, *Culture in Mind: Cognition, Culture, and the Problem of Meaning* (New York: Oxford University Press, 1996); J. G. Blair, "Interchange-

Modular thinking has had a successful history in America. It is responsible for the development of the assembly line and Taylorist innovations in scientific management, and it provides the foundational principles behind everything from the construction of shopping malls to the planning of school curricula. More central for our argument, the pervasive pragmatic modular approach to life permits Americans to avoid divisive ideological issues by visualizing the world around them as a machine that can be retooled, or taken apart and rebuilt, in order to achieve maximum efficiency. In other words, "the American Way became simply the common-sense way to get things done. . . . Americanism was the way of reason and nature."[9] Disagreements are not over principles, but over design. Though this mechanistic instrumental worldview may remove much of the magic from the cosmos, and though it certainly does not grasp complex social realities, it is not likely to arouse great passions either — and so is conducive to social peace.

It is especially striking that for Americans even the self is considered to be a kind of modular entity, capable of being reconfigured to fit into preferred life styles. This malleability is often decried as indicating American shallowness, or else praised as the postmodern triumph of the signifier.[10] But the American emphasis on perpetual self-transformation also serves the cause of unity, though perhaps not in the way Protestant moralists would prefer. This is because the search for identity is a notoriously solipsistic pursuit: such quests do not lead to

able Parts and the Organization of Life in the United States," in R. Kroes, ed., *The American Identity: Fusion and Fragmentation* (Amsterdam: Amerika Instituut, 1980); G. Gorer, *The American People: A Study in National Character* (New York: Norton, 1948).

[9] S. Berkovitch, "Fusion and Fragmentation: The American Identity," in Kroes, *The American Identity*, 27.

[10] J. Baudrillard, *America* (London: Verso, 1988).

revolution, but to harmless participation in the therapeutic, self-help, and twelve-step groups that have so mushroomed in America.[11] At the very worst, the search for an authentic self draws the most perplexed seekers toward immersion in the multitude of sects and cults that have always sprouted on American soil. Occasionally, it is true, these groups spiral into psychosis, as has occurred recently with the followers of Charles Manson, Jim Jones, and David Koresh and in the Heaven's Gate cult,[12] but generally these new religions are akin to the "healthy-minded," "once-born" faiths that William James found so characteristic of America. They typically affirm the goodness of all creation and preach accommodation with the world as it is, stressing mental discipline, while applying the optimistic American "can-do" attitude to spiritual uplift and practical self-betterment.[13] Membership in them is no more harmful than membership in any local PTA.

American faith in the power of individuals to change themselves is quite understandable as a product of the immigrant experience in combination with the Protestant ethos. Protestant sects believe that individuals can be spiritually trans-

---

[11] C. Lasch, *The Culture of Narcissism: American Life in an Age of Diminishing Expectations* (New York: Norton, 1978). Lasch's view of these groups is unrelentingly negative. For a more positive perspective, see R. Wuthnow, *Sharing the Journey: Support Groups and America's New Quest for Community* (New York: Free Press, 1994).

[12] C. Lindholm, *Charisma* (Oxford: Blackwell, 1990); R. Kanter, *Commitment and Community* (Cambridge: Harvard University Press, 1972). In their hierarchical structure and exclusive nature, these groups serve as rhetorical reversals of the American mainstream, which is one reason they create so much anxiety.

[13] W. James, *The Varieties of Religious Experience* (reprint, London: Penguin, 1982). For an account of modern "once born" movements, see C. Lindholm, "Crowds, Charisma and Altered States of Consciousness," *Culture, Medicine and Psychiatry* 16 (1992): 287–310.

formed through disciplined, virtuous action in this world. For most of the original settlers immigration to America was just such a transformative action, a voluntary pilgrimage in search of the City on a Hill. In secular garb, this model continues to hold: becoming an American is a kind of conversion experience. The newcomer "is not required to learn a philosophy," Daniel Boorstin notes, "so much as to rid his lungs of the air of Europe."[14] This point is not invalidated by the fact that more recent immigrants, male and female, rid their lungs of the air of China, India, and Africa. For all of these newcomers, past and present, whatever their race, creed, or cultural background, America has been the "Mother of Exiles. From her beacon — hand glows world — wide welcome."[15] The content of the glowing welcome offered by the Statue of Liberty is not a dogma, but an opportunity. America presents itself as a place where newcomers can achieve their dreams, free at last from the chains of tradition, class, and history — a place where, in the words of Bill Clinton, "you should be given a chance to go as far as your God-given ability will take you."[16]

For the zealous believer of colonial times, the end sought through migration to America was a passage into heaven, a goal requiring arduous self-examination and participation in the proper sectarian community. For the modern entrepreneur, the goal is likely to be far more mundane: owning one's

---

[14] D. Boorstin, "How Belief in the Existence of an American Theory Has Made a Theory Superfluous," in R. Boorstin, *Daniel J. Boorstin Reader*, 770. Compare Emerson's lament, cited in G. W. Pierson, "The M-Factor in American History," *American Quarterly* 15 (1962): 289: "Can we never extract the tapeworm of Europe from the brain of our countrymen?"

[15] These are the words of the poet Emma Lazarus inscribed on the base of the Statue of Liberty.

[16] Quoted in J. Hochschild, *Facing Up to the American Dream: Race, Class, and the Soul of the Nation* (Princeton, N.J.: Princeton University Press, 1995), 18.

own business and acquiring a house in an exclusive suburb. Whether what they sought was spiritual or material, immigrants to America have worried little about conceptual consistency or a systematic organization of principles. Central instead is a belief that individuals have the capacity, through personal effort, dogged discipline, and creative innovation, to leave the past behind, to pursue happiness, and to become whatever their potential allows. Only in America would the Army call on its recruits to "be all you can be."

We can feel the heady appeal of this transformative aspect of American life in a letter sent by a French migrant to California during the Gold Rush:

> In the midst of this world of adventurers, who change their occupation as often as they do their shirt, egad, I did as the others. As mining did not turn out remunerative enough, I left it for the town, where in succession I became a typographer, a slater, plumber, etc. In consequence of thus finding out that I am fit for any sort of work, I feel less of a mollusk and more of a man.[17]

For such adventurous souls, America indeed offered — and continues to offer — an opportunity for taking on a new and better identity, for making a mollusk into a human being.

Of course, we must immediately recall that the promise was not always realized. Many immigrants were, and still are, isolated in ghettos and relegated to the lowest and most demeaning job categories;[18] the figure of Jay Gatsby further reminds us that success has not always led either to happiness or to acceptance. We must also remember that nonwhite ethnic back-

---

[17] C. Degler, *Out of Our Past: The Forces That Shaped Modern America* (New York: Harper, 1959), 127.

[18] See L. Lamphere, ed., *Structuring Diversity: Ethnographic Perspectives on the New Immigration* (Chicago, University of Chicago Press, 1992).

grounds have continued to be prejudiced against despite the ethic of egalitarianism. But for now we simply wish to stress the remarkable fact that the never-ending efforts at self-manufacture by successive waves of immigrants did not result, as one would have expected, in a plethora of different identities and conflicting world views. Instead, the perpetual efforts of immigrants to recast themselves always led in the same direction, to Americanization. Tocqueville formulated the point with characteristic verve: "American society appears animated because men and things are constantly changing; it is monotonous because all these changes are alike."[19] Jealous protection of "traditional" aspects on the "ethnic" side of the hyphen has made little actual difference in the results of the transformations of immigrants. Pursuing the same dream, Americans end up looking and thinking very much alike, no matter where they came from.[20] From this point of view, the postmodern "triumph of the signifier" is just another moment in the nervous, energetic, repetitive drama of American culture, as each striving individual seeks to become "all you can be" through ceaseless labor, accumulation, consumption, and display.

[19] Tocqueville, *Democracy in America*, 614.

[20] M. Lind, *The Next American Nation: The New Nationalism and the Fourth American Revolution* (New York: Free Press, 1995); M. Waters, *Ethnic Options: Choosing Identities in America* (Berkeley: University of California Press, 1990).

Sacred values

The ambiguity, practicality, and changeability of American conceptual equipment might seem to imply an absence of core substantive beliefs. Nothing could be further from the truth. As we have already implied, American pragmatism is actually rooted in deeply held anti-authoritarian, individualistic, egalitarian, activist ideals, which privilege personal choice, flexibility, and technical efficiency in the pursuit of success, however success is defined. While obscurity and contradiction might undermine a logical argument, they have no such effect on faith, and America, as G. K. Chesterton observed, is "a nation with the soul of a church."[1]

In describing Americanism as a kind of religion, we are again following Durkheim, who argued that, contrary to popular opinion, one cannot define religion by belief in God or, indeed, by any particular theology, but only sociologically, by the division of the world into the sacred and the profane — two realms that are set apart from and opposed to each other.[2] The profane, Durkheim argues, is above all associated with egoism — and in particular with the economy. The sacred, in contrast, is collective and consists of a group's shared beliefs and practices. Only through active participation in such a sacred community, Durkheim argues, can separate individuals experience the transcendence that comes with immersion in something larger than the self. And only such an experience can inculcate the ethic of self-sacrifice that morality and social life require.

Although he developed his thesis by way of an analysis of Australian Aborigines, Durkheim actually had in mind the transformative power of the nation, which he understood as

---

[1] G. K. Chesterton, *What I Saw in America* (New York: Dodd, Mead, 1922), 12.

[2] E. Durkheim, *The Elementary Forms of Religious Life* (reprint, Glencoe, Ill.: Free Press, 1965).

the contemporary form of society's collective worship of itself. In his formulation, the flag becomes the holy symbol of society, a sign of unity that citizens are willing to die for. The collective values and rituals of the nation are equally sacred; they provide the emotional basis for the participation, ethical commitment, and shared faith that stabilizes the social world. A Durkheimian formulation helps to account for the feelings Americans have about the Bill of Rights, the Constitution, and the Declaration of Independence. The aura of sacredness that surrounds these icons is only heightened by lack of detailed knowledge of their actual content. The secular religion of Americanism also has its places of pilgrimage, its shrines, its holidays, its rituals, its sacred texts and articles of faith. If the Pledge of Allegiance is not presently recited as much as it was, the words still have extensive currency; it is equally striking that every major sporting event begins with the national anthem, while social critics can still all too easily be termed "un-American." Lacking a national religion, America has made a religion of the nation.[3]

There are several reasons why this should be so. In the first place, America began in a spiritual quest, and the ideal of the nation as "God's country" has deep and lasting roots. More significant, where older nations can discover a sense of spiritual unity in their myths of origin, America, as the "first new nation" and as a conglomerate of immigrants, was obliged to

[3] The most important discussion of America's "civil religion" is R. Bellah, *The Broken Covenant: American Civil Religion in a Time of Trial*, 2d ed. (Chicago: University of Chicago Press, 1992). For more anthropological views, see W. L. Warner et al., *Yankee City*, abridged ed. (New Haven: Yale University Press, 1963), and M. Singer, "The Melting Pot: Symbolic Ritual or Total Social Fact?" in H. Varenne, ed., *Symbolizing America* (Lincoln: University of Nebraska Press, 1986). S. Bercovitch, *Rites of Assent: Transformations in the Symbolic Construction of America* (London: Routledge, 1992) offers a literary perspective.

look instead to the revolutionary past for its sacred charter. Early American history has thus lost its specificity, and instead serves to transform reality into a shared moral drama that draws all its diverse citizenry into a mythic American collective identity. As the literary critic Secvan Bercovitch writes:

> Discrimination, poverty, alienation: figurally considered, such things were merely temporary, probational, like the obstacles encountered by the elect on their way to New Jerusalem. . . . Multiplicity itself became a chief argument for the basic unity of design. . . . All the fragmented aspects of life and thought in this pluralist society flowed into "America," the symbol of fusion and fragmentation entwined, and then outward again to each self-reliant unit of the culture.[4]

In this quasi-mystical worldview, reason and logic have little place; what does have a place is the affirmation of the goodness of America — the land of the free and the home of the brave, possessed of a sacred mission to save the world from tyranny and evil. In this sacralized universe, the motivations of Americans have been bathed in a halo of sanctity that sets them apart from and above the rest of the threatening outside world.

Americans' faith in their hallowed past and their deep sense of righteousness may sometimes seem arrogant and pious to outsiders, but these values provide a powerful cohesive force. They give citizens a proud feeling that they belong to a nation that is not only strong but also good, a place where "being all you can be" is morally right. Accordingly, citizens tend to assume that to be an American is to act instinctively in righteous

[4] S. Bercovitch, "Fusion and Fragmentation: The American Identity," in R. Kroes, ed., *The American Identity: Fusion and Fragmentation* (Amsterdam: Amerika Instituut, 1980), 26, 33, 36.

and ethical American ways. One of the informants in Alan Wolfe's recent survey made this point forcefully:

> People are inherently good and they can make the right decisions based on what's right and what's wrong, not necessarily because that's what their religion taught them. If you don't have religion, there's still right and wrong.[5]

All people naturally know, this American believes, what right and wrong are for themselves in their own particular circumstances, and everyone naturally wants to be moral and just. Davey Crockett's famous maxim — "Be sure you're right, then go ahead" — still has resonance for Americans.

From this moral perspective, what the society at large must do is allow each individual to follow his or her own innate sense of morality; all will then be well. Differences in preference are not to be argued with, but accepted: "A deep-seated belief in people's goodness enables middle-class Americans to accept the principle that . . . good people will always make the right kinds of choices."[6] Buoyed by their faith in the innate morality of themselves and others, and trusting in general goodwill, Americans, in the words of the philosopher George Santayana, are marked by "a ready jocoseness, a democratic amiability, and a radiant conviction that there is nothing better than oneself."[7]

Of course, trusting that all innately good American citizens will make morally proper decisions greatly helps to maintain social peace. In a universe where "sincerity means commitment to the liberal-democratic, individualist ideals of the

---

[5] A. Wolfe, *One Nation, After All* (New York: Viking, 1998), 87.

[6] Ibid., 85.

[7] Quoted in G. W. Pierson, "The M-Factor in American History," *American Quarterly* 15 (1962): 287.

American Creed,"[8] there is little of substance for people to argue over; and since these creedal beliefs are nebulous, inarticulate, and pervasive anyway, it is almost impossible for most Americans even to imagine what serious debate over fundamental principles would entail. Vaguely counting on the general decency of others, and feeling themselves to partake equally in the same sacred national community, Americans also tend to be suspicious of strong opinions and of any sort of zealotry.[9] Telling anyone what to do, Americans feel, would be asserting moral superiority — a cardinal sin in an egalitarian ethos:[10]

> Above all moderate in their outlook on the world, [Americans] believe in the importance of leading a virtuous life but are reluctant to impose values they understand as virtuous for themselves on others; strong believers in morality, they do not want to be considered moralists.[11]

The value of moderation is expressed in a characteristic American stance of "moral minimalism," wherein "people pre-

[8] S. Huntington, *American Politics: The Promise of Disharmony* (Cambridge: Harvard University Press, 1981), 83.

[9] A 1987 Gallup poll reported that 44 percent of Americans would not like to live next door to a religious sectarian; in comparison, 11 percent would not like to live next to an African American.

[10] This is one reason why Americans prefer to complain anonymously to police when troubled by neighbors, rather than risking a confrontation. "[I]n seeing themselves as social or moral equals, as Americans believe they are, one rule of thumb is not to take any sort of superior attitude, and criticizing another's behavior certainly carries that connotation. Directly complaining to a neighbor can readily be seen as telling them what to do. When a personal show of superiority is culturally forbidden substituting the impersonal, yet legitimate, authority of local government and homeowner boards makes much sense." C. Perin, *Belonging in America: Reading between the Lines* (Madison: University of Wisconsin Press, 1988), 80.

[11] Wolfe, *One Nation, After All*, 278.

fer the least extreme reactions to offenses and are reluctant to exercise any social control against one another at all."[12] In other words, the 11th commandment is "Thou shalt not judge."[13] It may seem paradoxical that one of Americans' strongest moral values is a reluctance to impose moral values, but a moment's reflection will show that this is simply an expression of an individualistic faith that all persons ought to have the freedom to make their own fates without restraint from their neighbors; concomitantly, they, too, should not meddle with anyone else. In the past, this tolerant spirit suited the openness and rough egalitarianism of a frontier society;[14] today it correlates with the roomy and solipsistic world of the suburb, where there is usually no need for neighbors to confront one another, where it is even possible for members of the same household to have separate rooms, separate schedules, and separate meals and almost never come into contact.[15] The same ethic prevails in America's automated factories and construction sites, where workers focus on the task at hand and

[12] M. P. Baumgartner, *The Moral Order of a Suburb* (Oxford: Oxford University Press, 1988), 3. Following Riesman's analysis in *The Lonely Crowd*, Baumgartner believes the American ethic of avoidance is a result of social fragmentation associated with modernity. But she also notes that "moral minimalism" is in fact a dominant form of conflict resolution in many small-scale societies.

[13] Wolfe, *One Nation, After All*, 54.

[14] Tolerance in this instance means acceptance of small differences within a shared way of life rather than tolerance of alternative visions of societal order.

[15] For working-class and poor Americans, relationships tend to be more volatile and confrontational, a consequence of both somewhat differing attitudes and more constrictive social settings. For a recent ethnographic study of the complex relationship between class and concepts of self in America, see A. Kusserow, "The American Self Reconsidered: 'Soft' and 'Hard' Individualism in Manhattan and Queens" (Ph.D. diss., Harvard University, 1995).

avoid confrontations or even socializing. The motto is, "Do your own work and don't mess with anybody's shit."[16] Under these conditions of cultivated indifference, Americans interact smoothly with others so long as those others do not make demands on one's time and autonomy, or interfere in the efficient completion of one's work.

In part, the social trust and nonjudgmental tolerance of Americans are a legacy of the original Protestant covenanted church, now transferred to the larger secularized social world, where the primary goals are no longer sanctity and salvation, but simply being "well liked" and "getting along well with others." Socialization toward these ends can be seen at work particularly clearly in the American school system. Popular students are elected as student body leaders whose job is to "represent" their fellows, while children are graded on the quality of their "citizenship" — and on whether they "cooperate well." Students are also expected to take part in extracurricular activities that oblige them to participate together on a voluntary basis. Team sports are highly valued as an expression of "school spirit" and local pride, allowing gifted individuals to show off their personal talents while also learning to work together. These institutions have nothing to do with formal education, everything to do with learning how to cooperate peacefully in a fluid entrepreneurial society of competitive individualists.[17]

---

[16] G. Genier, A. Stepick, et al., "On Machines and Bureaucracy: Controlling Ethnic Interaction in Miami's Apparel and Construction Industries," in L. Lamphere, ed., *Structuring Diversity: Ethnographic Perspectives on the New Immigration* (Chicago: University of Chicago Press, 1992), 86.

[17] P. Smith, *As a City upon a Hill: The Town in American History* (New York: Knopf, 1966). It may seem a long leap from Puritanism to high school sports, but that would be to forget that it was New England Protestants who invented baseball, football, and basketball with specific concern for inculcating moral values in their youth. For more on this topic,

The characteristic American smiley-faced "niceness," so often commented on with various degrees of amusement or condescension by foreign visitors, is another expression of the pressure among egalitarian free agents to find the middle ground so as to "get along" with unknown others. In contrast to their class- and tradition-bound European cousins, who are far more formal and private in their expression of emotion, the typical American self-presentation of amiable informality is appropriate for a "new realm of uncertain boundaries, in an affable, communal world which, strictly speaking, was neither public nor private: a world of first names, open doors, front porches, and front lawns."[18] In this changeable and open public realm, an easygoing, friendly demeanor allows strangers to negotiate a social minefield where there are no clear status markers and where authority is decentralized and relatively weak; this unstable and potentially threatening universe is made livable by the expectation that one's own friendliness and helpfulness will be returned.[19]

Of course, it is no secret that generalized niceness can mask real differences of opinion and interest. But such masking is recognized to be a necessary precaution in a universe of independent and often rivalrous coequals. As the mayor of an American town observed:

---

see D. H. Fischer, *Albion's Seed: Four British Folkways in America* (Oxford: Oxford University Press, 1989).

[18] D. Boorstin, "Palaces of the Public," in R. Boorstin, ed. *The Daniel J. Boorstin Reader* (New York: Modern Library, 1995), 131.

[19] For the American requirement to be friendly, see H. Varenne, "Creating America," in Varenne, *Symbolizing America*; S. Kalberg, "The Sociology of Friendliness" (unpublished manuscript, n.d.); N. Rosenblum, *Membership and Morals: The Personal Uses of Pluralism in America* (Princeton, N.J.: Princeton University Press, 1998).

We are a deeply fragmented community. We're *nice* to each other so much of the time we get the idea that's all there is. But since the problems and misunderstandings remain pretty consistent year after year, I have to assume we don't actually like each other as much as we claim to. Maybe nice is what you have to be or you'd be swinging at each other all the time.[20]

Social peace is served as well by another aspect of "getting along" and being "nice" — the requirement not to act as if one were superior to one's fellow Americans. Perhaps the worst insult that can be hurled at an American is, "Who do you think you are?"[21] To avoid this accusation, in their ordinary interactions Americans neither demand nor offer any sort of deference, and collude together to present a casual, "nice," friendly, and transparently sincere demeanor, which is suitable for almost all occasions.[22]

This equalizing etiquette has a long history. From colonial times, "extreme inequalities of material condition were joined to an intense concern for equality of esteem" as rich and poor "wore similar clothing and addressed each other by first names. They worked, ate, laughed, played and fought together on a footing of equality."[23] Despite real distinctions in wealth, most Americans remain as scrupulous as their colonial prede-

---

[20] The mayor of Hamilton, Ohio, quoted in P. Davis, *Hometown: A Portrait of an American Community* (New York: Simon and Shuster, 1982), 17.

[21] M. Moffatt, *Coming of Age in New Jersey* (New Brunswick, N.J.: Rutgers University Press, 1992), describes the dire consequences of being accused of snobbism among undergraduates at Rutgers.

[22] For a brilliant analysis of the techniques of American public culture, see E. Goffman, *The Presentation of Self in Everyday Life* (New York: Anchor Books, 1959).

[23] Fischer, *Albion's Seed*, 754.

cessors in cloaking authority relations with the trappings of equality. On the job, subordinates are "team members," whose "consent" and "cooperation" are "requested" by their "supervisors,"[24] who are, at least in theory, "glad-handed, extravert, mindful of first names, seeing their subordinates in their shirt sleeves and with their feet on the desk, democratically obscene in their language, with private interests, if any, simple and within the reach of all."[25] Meanwhile, at home it is perfectly acceptable to have servants or to go to an elite school, but not to put the servants in livery or to have a genteel accent. The American outfit of blue jeans and work shirt can be worn by everyone, demonstrating that even the richest are workers at heart, while in restaurants, waiters often cheerily introduce themselves by name to their customers. In short, it is politically correct to be rich and powerful just so long as one does not make claims to be different and better.

This distaste for snobbery and the related demand for equal recognition regardless of actual hierarchical distinctions was at work when a nineteenth-century scavenger testified in court, "When he first observed the *gentleman* he was filling his dung-cart,"[26] and in the horrified report from the British consul in Boston in 1840 that servant girls "are, when walking the streets, scarcely to be distinguished from their employers."[27] Such democratizing affirmations of equality and respect would be ludi-

---

[24] See D. Potter, "Individuality and Conformity," in M. McGiffert, ed., *The Character of Americans* (Homewood, Ill.: Dorsey Press, 1964), for these, and more, examples.

[25] G. Gorer, *The American People: A Study in National Character* (New York: Norton, 1948), 40.

[26] N. Harris, "American Manners" in L. S. Luedtke, ed., *Making America: The Society and Culture of the United States* (Chapel Hill: University of North Carolina Press, 1992), 150.

[27] D. Boorstin, "A Democracy of Clothing," in R. Boorstin, *Daniel J. Boorstin Reader*, 231.

crous in Europe, but they have long been standard in America, where "individuals confront one another in their individual identities and not as members of broader solidarities or groups."[28] Demands for personal recognition and for equality in interaction are a powerful symbolic mechanism that allows Americans to ignore invidious differences, and to believe that they are indeed "created equal" and united in a community based on caring rather than on power.[29]

The family both expresses and inculcates this ethos. Americans believe that the family is a locus of "diffuse, enduring solidarity" where unity is achieved not through rules and regulations or through coercion and charisma but by means of consensus and affection.[30] In the prototypical middle-class American family setting, the father is hardly a commanding patriarchal authority figure. Along with other family members, he must use negotiation and example, not command, to get his way. The relative absence of paternal power in suburban middle-

[28] A. Seligman, *The Idea of Civil Society* (New York: Free Press, 1992), 155.

[29] That these values are, indeed, deeply held has been confirmed by any number of psychological tests. For instance R. D'Andrade, *The Development of Cognitive Anthropology* (Cambridge: Cambridge University Press, 1995) finds that for Americans, "the strong dislike of being controlled by others and being treated as an inferior person . . . comes through strongly. The opposite of this kind of domination is found in the sub-clusters of mutual caring and mutual sharing, in which an egalitarian relationship is maintained at the same time each person in the relationship both gives and receives material and emotional resources" (88).

[30] See D. Schneider, *American Kinship: A Cultural Account* (Chicago: University of Chicago Press, 1980), for this model, abstracted from his intensive study of the structure and symbolism of American kinship. Of course, there are class, ethnic, and racial variations; for example, poor black families often have extended family structures, in which kinship — both real and fictive — is used to knit together a loose alliance of mutual aid. On this, see C. Stack's classic, *All Our Kin: Strategies for Survival in a Black Community* (New York: Harper and Row, 1975).

class America correlates with the very real independence of children, who have their own private rooms, property, and incomes, and have almost no long-term interests to bring them together with their parents. In keeping with the overriding ethic of autonomy, American children generally expect to be paid for their labor around the home, and can even be fired if their work is not up to par. In this businesslike atmosphere, the only thing holding the family together is love. This fragile emotional bond is, however, supposed to be enough: love is believed to have the power to dissolve hierarchy and to bind independent individuals together in an egalitarian community of unselfish mutuality.[31]

The familial anti-authoritarian expression of positive emotion has great resonance and extension in American culture. For Americans, "unsmiling subservience produces discomfort, unsmiling arrogance, fear and hostility. The emotional egalitarianism of America demands that all relationships shall bear some resemblance to those of love and friendship."[32] The expansion of familial affection into the public sphere is especially important, since it can resolve the tension between freedom and participation. This is a tension that Americans feel especially strongly. In most other cultures, the community precedes the individual, who finds a place within it. In contrast, for Americans, "individualism is natural, community problematical. *Society has to be built.*"[33]

[31] For statements about the American family, see C. Lasch, *Haven in a Heartless World* (New York: Basic Books, 1977), and (in a very different mood) E. Erikson, *Childhood and Society* (New York: Norton, 1950). On love as the central metaphor of American culture, see H. Varenne, *Americans Together: Structured Diversity in an American Town* (New York: Teachers College Press, 1977).

[32] Gorer, *American People*, 133.

[33] Varenne, *Americans Together*, 70 (emphasis in original). Cf. B. Bailyn, *The Ideological Origins of the American Revolution* (Cambridge: Harvard

This characteristic American viewpoint correlates with the indigenous "sect spirit" that Max Weber found so remarkable. To recapitulate, for Protestant sectarians, society was a moral corporation knitted together by voluntary agreements among independent and equal agents, all bearing responsibility for their acts, and each seeking personal salvation. These spiritual seekers believed that only participation in a moral community could accomplish God's work on earth, and so they were strongly compelled to join a church. Yet despite the necessity of belonging to a sacred association, the individual's conscience always had priority; the church community was bound together only by the loyalties of kindred enlightened spirits. In practice, this meant that the authority of any spiritual community could be contested, as members sought comrades and preachers more to their taste, and searched for truth within their own hearts, outside of formal theology. The physical and social openness of America exaggerated this tendency, so that the history of American churches is one of continual schism.

The proliferation of sects and cults is a reflection of American spiritual individualism, as charismatic figures find God's message not through texts but through introspection and personal illumination. In America, even Catholicism has developed a "charismatic" strand.[34] Pentecostalism, the world's fastest-growing faith and the paradigmatic American contribution to world religions, takes personal rapture as its spiritual core. In American fashion, it is then affirmed that ecstatic experience and spiritual love will spread contagiously to undo distinctions and bind all of humanity together in eternal bliss.

University Press, 1967), and J. R. Pole, *The Pursuit of Equality in American History* (Berkeley: University of California Press, 1978).

[34] For a recent analysis, see T. Csordas, *The Sacred Self: A Cultural Phenomenology of Charismatic Healing* (Berkeley: University of California Press, 1994).

This claim is not new: the same millennarian and antinomian enthusiasms lay behind the attacks on formal church hierarchies during the Great Awakening. The decentralized congregational form, so characteristic of America, is an attempt to maintain a modicum of church solidarity in the face of never-ending pressures toward dissolution of formal authority in favor of personal revelation.[35]

Just as congregational church organization was a response to the independence of Americans, so was the remarkably fluid and decentralized structure of American government, as states, counties, and towns fought for the dubious loyalties of an ambulatory and anti-authoritarian citizenry.[36] Let us note once again that this vision of American political culture runs counter to Tocqueville's image of the isolated and impotent individual, purportedly ready to submit to a tyrannical state unless trained to citizenship through participation in local level organizations. Rather, we take Weber's view that Americans are predisposed to resist attempts to impose authority from any direction. Community, for Americans, is a moral good, but it can never be dictated, and can be arrived at only through the voluntary cooperation of equals. Government is valued only insofar as it furthers the higher end of the individual's salvation; otherwise Americans follow Walt Whitman's admonition — "Resist much, obey little."[37]

The same underlying principles continued to operate even

[35] See R. Wuthnow, *Sharing the Journey: Support Groups and America's New Quest for Community* (New York: Free Press, 1994), on the contemporary spread of small groups as the modern expression of the same process.

[36] The uniquely American educational system has the same source and structure. On this, see M. Trow, "American Higher Education: 'Exceptional' or Just Different?" in B. Shafer, eds., *Is America Different? A New Look at American Exceptionalism* (Oxford: Oxford University Press, 1991).

[37] Whitman, quoted in Gorer, *American People*, 34.

when communities ceased to be based on overtly religious faith. The businessmen who founded American towns in the great drive westward in the 1830s typically combined the profit motive with fervent civic boosterism and strong community pride. Competing with other new towns for settlers, these entrepreneur-politicians promised newcomers a better life and great possibilities for the future; each town was promoted as the secular equivalent to the Puritan City on a Hill, capable of providing a potential commercial, cultural, and spiritual center. Newcomers restlessly searching for a viable future attached themselves to these mushrooming towns with loyalties that were "intense, naïve, optimistic and quickly transferable."[38] Full of hope and ambition, these mobile Americans sought to construct or discover a place where they could achieve success, build homes, raise their children, and participate with their neighbors in a moral community. The role of the central government was simply to facilitate this search, providing goods and services as required.

Despite great shifts in the economy, the same general ethos continues to pertain today. Americans still are amazingly mobile, searching both for personal success and for a meaningful association with others, while also resisting impositions upon their autonomy. Resistance is perhaps even more emotionally charged than ever, as more and more Americans spend their economic lives working in impersonal corporations where freedom is actually negligible. In radical contrast to the world of business, for those who have sought to build up or simply to belong to a voluntary association, the weak tie among members has been symbolized in the language that has always been used to strengthen and justify the equally fragile bond that unites the family and binds together charismatic congrega-

---

[38] D. Boorstin, "The Businessman as an American Institution," in R. Boorstin, *Daniel J. Boorstin Reader*, 117.

tions: "Boy and girl marry because they are in love. People live with people in communities because they love each other."[39]

The trope of love — or, minimally, of liking — allows competitive egalitarian individualists to conceptualize and experience immersion into the civic sphere. Within this cultural model, community members, like marriage partners, recognize one another as independent individuals who are bound together primarily by personal affection rather than by rules, laws, interests, or authority. Affection can cool and membership can shift, as in marriage, but the anti-authoritarian, individualistic notion of a voluntaristic community united by caring remains the same.[40] In love or in community, Americans reserve for themselves the right to continue to search for personal happiness through relations with others. Divorce, for example, is not an act of despair, but the prelude to a better and more fulfilling relationship. Communities are joined and left in the same spirit.

In this context we can understand the deep American "aversion to interest-based politics tout court. The classic democratic rationale for voluntary associations — as agents for identifying, expressing, and representing interests, and expanding the political agenda — has become anathema."[41] Interest-based groups are seen as illegitimate extensions of the instrumentality of the marketplace into what should be relations of car-

[39] Varenne, *Americans Together*, 194. In his classic account, *As a City upon a Hill*, Page Smith argues that the evocation of an emotional unity is an attempt by "cumulative" frontier communities typical of middle and western America to recapture the unity of the "covenanted" communities of the Puritan Northeast. But one need not invoke nostalgia; the tensions implicit in contradictory values of equality and community require some symbolic reconciliation.

[40] For an account of the ambiguities of neighborliness in America, see Perin, *Belonging in America*.

[41] Rosenblum, *Membership and Morals*, 150.

ing. Even American radicals can be romantic anarchists demanding a community of love rather than revolutionaries seeking to overturn the class hierarchy. The Knights of Labor wanted a cooperative national family of workers and owners; the counterculture of the 1960s almost universally demanded not an end to wealth, nor even income redistribution, but a more nurturing, caring society. In other words, American social critique has often been directed primarily against the inability of the political realm to offer the idealized comforts of a loving family, and only secondarily against the invidious realities of wealth and poverty.

Within this cultural framework, elected officials at every level must strive to demonstrate to their constituents that they are not egoists or supporters of special interests, but rather selfless servants of all the people. The relationship of official to citizen is symbolically enacted as the individual casts a ballot in the privacy and isolation of the voting booth, giving up personal political responsibility via a contract with the elected official, who then must act for all the individual voters within the aptly named Congress. This moral ideal of politics as a sacred social contract gives Americans a strong sense that their polity is not merely the locus of power seeking and deal making but rather the ethical center of a society where individuals, despite their differences, are joined together in a common humanity. This idealized vision of politics clearly has emotional power to draw Americans together. Equally, it has problems attached to it — to which we now turn.

Anti-politics in America

"Niceness" and its corollaries are but one side of a complex cultural picture. As S. M. Lipset has written:

> The lack of respect for authority, anti-elitism, and populism contribute to higher crime rates, school indiscipline, and low electoral turnouts. The emphasis on achievement, on meritocracy, is also tied to higher levels of deviant behavior and less support for the underprivileged. . . . Concern for the legal rights of accused persons and civil liberties in general is tied to opposition to gun control and difficulty in applying crime-control measures.[1]

In other words, American culture is charged with inner tensions. Such tensions cannot be avoided; they are intrinsic to any living society and give it its dynamism. What is unique is that Americans believe this should not be so. We have seen that many intellectuals believe that stress is destructive, that the nation is so frail that it will break apart as it loses its moral base.[2] These interrelated anxieties are symptoms of an American cultural belief that society is knit together only through the continuous and laborious reaffirmation of fragile moral and emotional bonds between autonomous individuals. Stability is felt by Americans to be precarious, and all contradictions are experienced as dangerous. In this chapter and the next, we explore the sources and directions of some characteristic loci of anxiety, and show why these do not really challenge the equilibrium of society.

Many readers will no doubt have been amazed and perhaps appalled at our Durkheimian characterization of the American

---

[1] S. M. Lipset, *American Exceptionalism: A Double-Edged Sword* (New York: Norton, 1996), 290. Cf. S. Huntington, *American Politics: The Promise of Disharmony* (Cambridge: Harvard University Press, 1981).

[2] R. Wilkinson, *The Pursuit of American Character* (New York: Harper and Row, 1988).

political realm as sacred, since a favorite modern American pastime is condemning the corruption and perfidy of professional politicians. With a typical absence of historical perspective, this disrespect is often regarded as a reflection of contemporary political alienation. In reality, modern politicians are treated with more respect than were their predecessors. In 1925, Nicholas Longworth, then Speaker of the House of Representatives, told an interviewer, "[W]e have been attacked, denounced, despised, hunted, harried, blamed . . . excoriated, and flayed. . . . From the beginning of the Republic it has been the duty of every free-born voter to look down on us."[3] Longworth also wryly noted that the president has always been more popular than the House, and he offered an astute analysis of why this has been so. The president's perennial popularity has sprung from the fact that he could make up his mind privately, and give an impression of speaking with one voice for the nation as a whole. The House, in contrast, is an arena where public dispute takes place, interests are aired, and combative disunion is evident. Americans, Longworth added, find this naked and noisy contestation over power disturbing and contemptible.

Americans do tend to idealize government at the national level, where the president symbolizes the solidarity of the whole, and at the local level, where the homey New England town meeting is the model for a voluntary community of neighborly equals.[4] For Americans, good politics is either among friends, or in the communion of the entire nation. However, the American public has a profound distaste for the realities of compromise, opposition and interest best exemplified in the

---

[3] N. Longworth, quoted in P. Boller, Jr., *Congressional Anecdotes* (Oxford: Oxford University Press, 1991), 15–16.

[4] We are indebted to R. Bellah et al., *Habits of the Heart* (New York: Harper and Row, 1985), for much of this argument.

plebeian and argumentative House. It is no surprise, then, that even when President Nixon had his lowest popularity rating, the popularity of the House sank even lower.[5] Longworth was right: the untidy operation of democracy in action tends to offend Americans.

Paradoxically, American distaste for practical political action is partly a logical consequence of the sacralization of the political realm. As Durkheim noted, the holy stands in radical contrast to the profane; in America, this means that the political is in symbolic opposition to the workings of the economy, where ruthless self-promotion is accepted as normal. Those who fail in the race either accept the logic of the marketplace and "prosecute themselves on its behalf,"[6] or they may claim that success is impossible for them, no matter how able they are, because the deck is stacked. But for all Americans, the market is a space for unfettered self-aggrandizement, not for sacred values.[7] Within this symbolic structure, "money becomes evil not when it is used to buy goods but when it is used to buy power."[8] The entrance of the economy into politics is felt to be a kind of pollution. Therefore, when politicians are seen to

---

[5] The Harris poll, quoted in Boller, *Congressional Anecdotes*, 16, gives the figures as 30 percent and 21 percent, respectively.

[6] K. Newman, *Falling from Grace: The Experience of Downward Mobility in the American Middle Class* (New York: Free Press, 1988), 75. For example, P. Bourgois, in his ethnography of East Harlem crack dealers, *In Search of Respect: Selling Crack in El Barrio* (Cambridge: Cambridge University Press, 1995), reports that his informants "attribute their marginal living conditions to their own psychological or moral failings" (54). One told him that "You have to do good for yourself in order to achieve. . . . The struggle's harder for the poor, but not impossible. . . . If I have a problem, it's because I brought it upon myself" (ibid.).

[7] J. Hochschild, *What's Fair? American Beliefs about Distributive Justice* (Cambridge: Harvard University Press, 1981).

[8] Huntington, *American Politics*, 38.

serve special interests, obey party policies, and kowtow to the influence of lobbies, they are abused for betrayal, and held up to public mockery. This could never happen if they were not put on moral pedestals in the first place.

Yet pork-barrel politics is inextricably embedded in American society. The institutional weakness of the central state, the separation of powers, and the internal divisions of the political parties allow American politicians to be less tied to national programs and more responsive to their constituents, but the same factors also make them reliant on partisan pressure groups and lobbies for financial and political backing. In America, "groups of voters elect representatives; individual voters do not."[9] Believing in a sacred polity removed from interests, the electorate cannot accept this reality; their opposition fuels repeated efforts to reform the electoral system and the constant public complaints about favoritism and corruption.

But there is yet another twist here, since individuals also hope to use the state for their own purposes. Tocqueville noted that in the egalitarian and competitive society of the United States:

> Men will freely admit the general principle that the power of the state should not interfere in private affairs, but as an exception, each one of them wants the state to help in the special matter with which he is preoccupied, and he wants to lead the government on to take action in his domain, though he would like to restrict it in every other direction.[10]

In other words, American objections to special interests are to interests that do not help *me*, and popular detestation of politicians is loathing of those who give favors to others, not to *me*.

[9] S. Issachaoff, "Polarized Voting and the Political Process," *Michigan Law Review* 90 (1992): 1859.

[10] A. de Tocqueville, *Democracy in America* (reprint, New York: Anchor Books, 1969), 672.

In sum, the combination of a sacralized polity with a decentralized institutional system that requires politicians to seek backing wherever they can find it means that the American public will always be in a turmoil over governmental corruption and injustice, will always feel a sense of betrayal and ambivalence toward their representatives. Yet high expectations of personal help from the state also mean that the same public will always seek to exploit government for what can be taken from it. This set of tensions leads to continual (usually futile) efforts at reform, but not to real social upheaval. No one wants to kill the sacred goose while it continues laying golden eggs.

The American view of politics as the realm of idealized community also helps to account for some of the ambiguities surrounding presidential politics. The American president has never been just a very successful politician: rather, he has symbolically represented, as argued, the whole nation, reaching beyond interest groups and the despised "party politics." The emotional expressiveness increasingly demanded of presidential figures is an indicator of this function, since the revelation and sharing of strong emotion demonstrates the president's common humanity — whereas concrete policies and interest politics are divisive. Voters who can sympathize with a president's personal tragedies and family trials feel a comforting communion. As a result, Americans are fascinated with the president's character and personal life. This obsession is magnified by the media revolution, which has exposed the activities at the political center to the view of ordinary Americans at the periphery. What had in previous generations been remote is now shimmering on the screen in everyone's living room; local politics, in contrast, have receded onto the back pages of provincial newspapers.

Unfortunately, familiarity with the president as a person necessarily breeds, if not contempt, at least a debunking of pretensions to extraordinary personal moral authority. However, this is not necessarily destructive to the unity of the society. Americans have never wanted their leaders to be saints, preferring them to be individuals like themselves — practical, personable rather than snobbish, tolerant, fair-minded, and willing to compromise. Premises of moral minimalism mean that, as long as the president is not perceived to be enslaved to party politics or special interests, or bent on overturning the sacred values of liberty, equality and justice, most Americans will forgive or ignore a great many venal sins. The recent unwillingness of Americans to impeach President Clinton, despite their skepticism about his personal integrity, is a striking example. Accordingly, while the Congress is bound to be disparaged for factionalism and power-seeking, even an erring president is likely to be supported, so long as he (or she) is able to voice the sacred values of Americans convincingly. This was what Nixon, having been proven by the Watergate break-in to be a cheater in the political game, was unable to do.

Thus, even though American ambivalences about the honor of politicians and the purity of the polity may be painful, they are neither resolvable nor destructive. Instead, such ambivalences serve as an enduring framework limiting and structuring discourse about the moral basis of American society. Without such a shared framework, no meaningful argument would be possible, and the polity truly would be in danger; with it, partisan energies are confined within a certain range, leading to periodic reforms rather than to violent conflict.

The sacralization of politics also lies behind another disturbing aspect of American culture: the propensity to demonize political opposition, and to sanctify one's own perspective. Because morally minimalist, modular-thinking Americans generally assume that policy disagreements are over technical detail rather than principle, they tend to remain aloof from politics. It is no accident, then, that political upheaval in America has to be accompanied by religious revivalism, arousing the passive citizenry by an emotionally charged "rediscovery" of the moral, egalitarian, and individualistic sacred values of the Founders.[11] The evangelical thrust of the Reagan revolution was part of this American tradition, linking distrust of "big government" with faith in America as a church headed by a fatherly every-man and based on voluntarism and free enterprise. During such periods of revivalism, political disagreement can be read as disrespect toward the sacred Founders and their sanctified texts. Acts taken to sully the symbols of the American faith are then likely to be regarded as heresy, and punished as such; hence the periodic witch hunts of "un-American" elements and the passionate fury aroused over such symbolic acts as flag-burning or the refusal to recite the Pledge of Allegiance.

This is a wholly American phenomenon. There is no such thing as "Britishism," and Britons opposing the policies of their queen and country do not thereby become "un-British": to the contrary, Anthony Blunt was a very British spy. Accusations of blasphemy can occur only in a society that believes itself to have a sacred foundation. Yet wrapping one's cause in the American flag can also promote changes for the better. This potential was best realized in the civil rights movement, which made the claim that America itself had become un-American in unfairly denying equal rights to some of its citizens. The successful appeal to core values gave the movement a moral authority it still retains, as was expressed symbolically by nam-ing a national holiday for Martin Luther King, Jr., thereby in-corporating him into the sacred pantheon.

Equally characteristic of America are single-issue political action groups. It is often said that the proliferation of single-issue politics in America indicates a disintegration of demo-

---

[11] Huntington, *American Politics*; S. Lipset, *The First New Nation: The United States in Historical and Comparative Perspective* (New York: Basic Books, 1963); W. McLoughlin, *Revivals, Awakenings, and Reforms* (Chicago: University of Chicago Press, 1978).

cratic consensus. This is mistaken: Americans have always been concerned less with political theory, more with what government can do for them in particular. Single-issue politics is an extension of this view, and shows, in general, a strong faith in the legitimacy and power of participation in the political arena. Such activist groups are also clear expressions of the sectarian character of American culture; they are voluntary associations of like-minded equals committed to what they believe to be a righteous cause. The content of the particular cause is less important sociologically than the form and function of these groups, which in all instances provide a small moral haven for individuals who feel themselves afloat in the vast sea of American life.[12] At the same time, political associations also provide a place for people to exercise choice, interact politically, moderate their views through cooperation and arbitration with others, and, in Tocqueville's terms, "learn to be citizens."

Most of these single-interest associations are peaceful enough, occupying themselves in such moral crusades as opposition to drunk driving or advocacy of more realistic and humane treatment of the mentally ill. In general, members are people who themselves are personally affected by the issues at hand. As lobbyists they press their cases in the political marketplace, and provide a positive demonstration of American grass-roots democracy working through the personally motivated actions of individuals acting together to influence the state. However, some of these groups may also use considerable violence in asserting their views. For example, anti-abortion and abortion rights groups seem to be at war with each other and sometimes with the society at large; militiamen, Afrocentricists, and white supremacists, among others, also engage in vicious rhetoric that tears at the social fabric.

While not downplaying the dangers of such heated dis-

---

[12] Tocqueville, *Democracy in America*, 605.

course and the occasional flare-ups of actual violence, we note that partisan invective is neither un-American nor novel. In any religion there are zealots who convince themselves that they are protecting fundamental truths, and therefore morally justified in taking extreme action against apostates. Violent though they may be, the sectarian devotion of these groups is always directed to the vague but potent principles that animate the faith of all Americans; they disagree over implementation rather than principle. In the debate over abortion, for example, both sides assert the central American value of the sacredness of the individual, differing only over whether the rights of the mother or those of the fetus should have priority. Militiamen similarly claim that they are upholding basic American values of freedom, while black and white supremacists alike argue over constitutional issues of equal rights under the law. Since none of these extremists, not even the most radical, wish to overthrow, or even to oppose, basic American principles of democracy, equality, and justice, their accusations pose no substantive ideological threat to the American faith. Despite their ferocity, they only serve to test the limits of its premises.

Nor do these groups pose any serious physical danger of overthrow or serious upheaval. In the larger American environment, fiery arguments are eventually dampened by the moderate attitudes of most Americans, who resist any group or individual making loud assertions or imperative calls to action. Americans like to believe, as noted, that "nice" people of good will, as all true Americans are assumed to be, ought to be able to reach a compromise and keep the social peace. Those who keep on refusing the path of compromise are castigated as troublemakers, demagogues, and even un-American. Since Americans are intolerant of intolerance, and hate being told what to feel or think, stimulation of "creedal passion"[13] is a

---

[13] The following analysis owes much to S. Huntington, *American Politics*, whose phrase this is.

politically desperate act that may solidify a core of true believers, but tends to discredit those who have recourse to it, and marginalize them outside the American mainstream.

It is within this context that we can understand the general American repudiation of the political demands made by special interest groups, such as gays, blacks, and feminists. Because Americans have a deep antipathy against all attempts to assert authority, "power concealed is power enhanced."[14] Those who command do so quietly, through private conversations and deals struck behind the scenes.[15] In contrast, relatively disenfranchised groups are obliged to use tactics of public confrontation to reach governmental officials and influence the electorate. Ironically, their noisy public protests undermine their own claims, since most Americans are offended at loud civic outcries, viewing them as a threat to social unity and harmony, and as unjust demands for special privileges for a particular interest group at the expense of the individuals who make up the community at large. However, activists are not the only ones to have felt this marginalizing effect; it operates as well within the center. The great modern example here is the short but rabid career of Senator Joe McCarthy, but we can see lesser instances in the rapid deflation of the more fervent preaching of the Republican revolution and the loss of support occasioned by Bob Dole's attempt to gain the presidency by moving toward the radical religious right.[16]

Cultural ambivalence about ardent political activism also lies behind another aspect of American politics that has caused

---

[14] Ibid., 76.

[15] Conspiracy theories are symbolic expressions of public awareness of this reality.

[16] Cf. S. Bruce, *The Rise and Fall of the New Christian Right: Conservative Protestant Politics in America, 1978–1988* (Oxford: Oxford University Press, 1990).

much hand-wringing. This is the low rate of voter participation, which is thought to indicate deep alienation from the political process. Negative media coverage is often blamed for this phenomenon, and negative campaign advertisements are also taken to be culprits in "turning off" the electorate. But American voter turnout has not normally been particularly high. This is partly because America is the most democratic of all nations: Americans are asked to vote more than are citizens of any other country.[17] There are over a million elections during a four-year period in the United States. Americans elect even judges and prosecutors, who are appointed for life in European countries, and they are asked to vote for any number of bond issues and amendments to local, state, and national laws. Even the Constitution can be amended by popular vote. The very excess of democratic choice undermines voter enthusiasm.[18]

This is clear enough. Less noted is the fact that voter apathy is the converse of the occasional moralizing upsurges of sectarian fervor we noted above. Americans have a taken-for-granted faith in the sacred objects and institutions of their nation, but, unless personally affected by a political upheaval, most of them do not want to experience the intense polarizing passions that agitate true believers. Such emotions are imprudent; they interfere with the necessary daily task of simply getting along with one's neighbors. We have also seen that what is normal in business is corruption in politics, and a corrupt politician is an abomination who has betrayed the sacred trust. Yet "abuse" is omnipresent, given the actual nature of the political system. Because political action carries such an ambiguous charge for Americans, many prefer to leave it to politicians and

---

[17] Lipset, *American Exceptionalism*, 43–44.

[18] Ibid., p. 45 points out that only Switzerland has an equivalent number of elections, and it has an equally low voter turnout.

their acolytes, who are experts at passionate advocacy and moralizing rhetoric — skills ordinary citizens do not greatly admire.[19]

Lack of participation also can signify relative satisfaction with things as they are. The widespread and rapid appearance and disappearance of single-issue pressure groups makes it clear that when confronted by matters they feel are personally relevant, Americans do become politically active. But when nothing particular concerns them, voters are content to remain quiet, occupying themselves with more pleasurable and more edifying nonpolitical activities, while letting the professional politicians do the dirty work of negotiating with various interest groups. However much one may wish for more public political activism, its relative absence is no surprise in a society that favors independence and anti-authoritarianism and surrounds politics with an aura of moral ambiguity. Furthermore, worry needs to be contextualized by remembering that the presence of popular political fervor by no means indicates a stable society; very often, the contrary is the case — as in Weimar Germany where impeccably high figures for voter turnout were merely a preface to the Nazi takeover.[20] Low voter turnout may be less a cause for concern than a reason for mild celebration.

---

[19] N. Rosenblum, *Membership and Morals: The Personal Uses of Pluralism in America* (Princeton, N.J.: Princeton University Press, 1998).

[20] R. Dahrendorf, *Society and Democracy in Germany* (New York: Anchor Books, 1969), chap. 21.

Ambivalence about association

American reluctance to participate in political action extends into associational life at large; this aversion is presently at the forefront of public attention. Contemporary excesses of individualism are such, according to Robert Putnam, that America is losing its social capital.[1] Putnam is here drawing on the conceptual armory of his important and much praised *Making Democracy Work*; this book contends that economic success and political development in the north as compared to the south of Italy resulted from the prior presence of communal solidarities.[2] It is this discovery that makes Putnam so appalled to discover that Americans now "bowl alone" — at once a fact about the decline of bowling leagues and a metaphor for a more generalized lack of involvement. The loss of trust that results looks set, according to Putnam, to undermine the economy — even, perhaps, to occasion political conflict.

Two words of warning need to be offered before turning to our own rather different analysis of group life in America.

---

[1] R. Putnam, "Bowling Alone," *Journal of Democracy* 6 (1995): 65–78, and "The Strange Disappearance of Civic America," *American Prospect* 24 (1996): 34–48.

[2] R. Putnam, *Making Democracy Work: Civic Traditions in Modern Italy* (Princeton, N.J.: Princeton University Press, 1993). The stimulation provided by this book should not lead to any general acceptance of its argument, which has been convincingly disputed by F. Sabetti, "Path Dependency and Civic Culture," *Politics and Society* 24 (1996): 19–44. For one thing, its historical account is flawed. The south of Italy was ruled by the Normans, but so was England, which is generally taken, not least by Tocqueville, as a bastion of liberal democracy. In fact, a culture relatively open to democracy in the south was probably destroyed from above, and in the nineteenth century at that. For another, the whole notion of comparing local government in northern and southern Italy is obviated by the fact that the units chosen in the north had historical roots, while those in the south did not. In a nutshell, Putnam does not bring to his views on America the authority of a universally accepted expert on civic affairs.

First, Putnam's claim that participation in group life has fallen off has been subjected to withering criticism, as should be his claim that this is largely caused by an excessive number of hours watching television.[3] His list of associations is, in fact, highly selective. For one thing, his earliest estimates turn out not to be correct. The survey on which he relied excluded memberships in service clubs and PTAs between 1989 and 1994: adding these back effectively wipes out the decline previously claimed for the two decades to 1994.[4] For another, a multitude of other contacts and associations are also missed, as are the widespread spiritual and therapeutic groups where many Americans find a form of community.[5] Putnam discounts such groups on the grounds that they do not further "practice in democracy." This narrow, rather patronizing view is mistaken. Such groups can be politicized; in any case, they are certainly socializing entities.

There is also a theoretical point to be made. Although Putnam considers himself a Tocquevillian, the French analyst's view of associational life is more ambiguous and complex than Putnam allows. Tocqueville did worry that apolitical American individuals might be so concerned with their self-interest as to ignore the common good, a tendency he thought might be countered by the training in citizenship provided by local-level

[3] E. C. Ladd, "The Data Just Don't Show Erosion of America's Social Capital," *Public Perspective* 7 (1996): 2, 5–6; M. Schudson, "What If Civic Life Didn't Die?" *American Prospect* 25 (1996): 17–20; G. Petticino, "Civic Participation and American Democracy," *Public Perspective* 7 (1996): 27–30. Cf. S. Verba, K. L. Schlozman, and H. E. Brady, *Voice and Equality: Civic Voluntarism in America* (Cambridge: Harvard University Press, 1995).

[4] A. Wolfe, *One Nation, After All* (New York: Viking, 1998), 252–53.

[5] R. Wuthnow, *Sharing the Journey: Support Groups and America's New Quest for Community* (New York: Free Press, 1994), 4, notes that four of every ten Americans now belong to self-help groups.

organizations. But there is another side to Tocqueville's analysis — one that reveals the French nobleman wary of democracy. The habit of political association, Tocqueville stresses,
will lead to the practice of forming civil associations — and this
is profoundly to be desired since it will *depoliticize* much of
social life. Thus the proliferation of American associations at
one and the same time takes us toward and away from politics,
a typically Tocquevillian paradox.[6] If Tocqueville is scarcely the
modern democrat that Putnam assumes him to be, this is not
to say that his interest in depoliticization is altogether unrealistic. For a further weakness of Putnam's analysis is its failure to
consider malign groups — a point neatly made by noting that
the convicted Oklahoma City bomber Timothy McVeigh was
an active participant in a bowling league.[7]

What matters still more than these criticisms is the need to
move altogether away from the terms of the debate that Putnam has inspired so as to place the ambivalence that Americans feel about associations at the center of attention. Let us
begin by critically extending an element in Tocqueville's analysis of associations missed by contemporary debate.The characteristic American elaboration of voluntary groups was best
understood, in Tocqueville's view, as an effort to establish
a personal identity and a place of comfort and community

---

[6] S. Holmes, "Tocqueville and Democracy," in D. Copp, J. Hampton, and
J. E. Roemer, eds., *The Idea of Democracy* (Cambridge: Cambridge University Press, 1993).

[7] Nancy Rosenblum's sophisticated treatment of civil associations in America makes a truly Tocquevillian point about malign groups, such as mili-
tias: while it is wildly mistaken to imagine that group life always promotes
democracy, very often the worst violence is committed by individuals who
act alone — while fanaticism is often contained in part by some kind of
membership. N. Rosenblum, *Membership and Morals: The Personal Uses
of Pluralism in America* (Princeton, N.J.: Princeton University Press,
1998), chap. 8 and Conclusion.

within the homogenizing and competitive world of the United States. But these groups, albeit often "artificial and arbitrary," are not devoid of a moral content.[8] American voluntary associations unite, as noted, for an almost infinite myriad of practical, recreational, religious, therapeutic, and educational purposes, but in all cases, the "sect spirit" impels members to believe that they are gathered together not for instrumental reasons but rather for the sake of love or mutual caring — while still using the group to further their own personal goals. In this, voluntary associations are parallel to the nurturing sacred realm of the family, and stand in contrast to the hard-hearted world of the marketplace, in which affection is supposed to have no place.[9]

Of course, there are variations along a continuum here. Condominium associations, for example, are convened for practical matters, and considerable painful conflict may occur among members; in contrast, participants in a self-help group are expected to give "unconditional support" to one another. But, ideally at least, disagreement within voluntary associations is kept to a minimum. "It doesn't matter whether the members of a community are objectively alike," the French anthropologist Hervé Varenne notes, "as long as they agree not to insist on expressing whatever differences may indeed exist." He found this to be so much the case that "some of my informants could literally be brought to tears if someone they considered

[8] A. de Tocqueville, *Democracy in America* (reprint, New York: Anchor Books, 1969), 605.

[9] This is not to say that Americans do not attempt to turn their places of business into a communities of friends. Sports clubs, company picnics, and the like are management efforts to erase the gap between work and community; informal coffee klatches serve the same purpose for individuals. But, although some Americans prefer the structured workplace to the demands of home, most attempts to humanize work have not been especially convincing.

close to them appeared to seriously disagree with them."[10] In contrast to the competitive hierarchies of business, events within voluntary associations are usually "engineered in such a way that a large number of people [are] involved in arriving at a course of action and responsibility [is] diffused throughout the community."[11] This coincides with a concerted effort to avoid the appearance of superiority; leadership should not be sought, but must be "forced" onto activist members, who always claim to be sacrificing themselves for the sake of the cause.

The agreement not to disagree, to mute upsetting differences within the group, is conducive to social peace, although it leads neither to the sort of political activism that Putnam favors nor to exactly the sort of equilibrium proposed in Tocqueville's two-sided theory. And there are further unexpected and potentially negative consequences that also flow from this constellation of beliefs. Members of American voluntary associations believe themselves to be united by shared caring; they are good people and good citizens, acting in a familial fashion, as "everybody" should act. In fact, it is common for Americans to refer to one's own group as "everybody," which "mediates the group in its aloneness with the rest of society by denying the relevance, if not the existence, of alternatives; outside of everybody there is nobody."[12] But the attribution of virtuous motives to one's own group necessarily implies, as Freud made us aware, the demonization of others.[13] Americans do

---

[10] H. Varenne, *Americans Together: Structured Diversity in an American Town* (New York: Teachers College Press, 1977), 205, 92.

[11] E. Hatch, *The Biography of a Small Town* (New York: Columbia University Press, 1979), 234.

[12] Varenne, *Americans Together*, 95.

[13] S. Freud, *Group Psychology and the Analysis of the Ego* (New York: Norton, 1959).

tend to be suspicious of the motivations of members of other groups, who may, they think, only be pretending to be decent and caring persons in order to further their pernicious special interests against the sacred well-being of the whole. For example, college students typically describe their own group as a bunch of friends, while other groups are disparaged as "cliques." Similarly, American social activists see themselves as selflessly trying to draw people into the community, while their opponents describe them as power-hungry and exclusionary.[14] Note, too, that in foreign policy issues, Americans tend to portray everyone but themselves as nationalistic and self-interested, a moralistic attitude that infuriates allied leaders.

The tension between idealized "us" and demonized "them" manifests itself at every level of American culture. Survey research on the leading members of a variety of influence blocs — labor leaders, businesspeople, feminists, bankers, farmers, media people, blacks, and students — shows that in general their ideals are the same as the ideals of the public at large.[15] But all — the weak and the strong alike — disagree about who *really* has influence: none see themselves as having power, all see power as unfairly grabbed by others, and all see "themselves as the victims not of a system deaf to all groups but of a system that 'plays favorites.'"[16] Since one's own group really represents "everybody," it follows that only one's own

[14] Hatch, *Biography of a Small Town*.

[15] S. Verba and G. Orren, *Equality in America: The View from the Top* (Cambridge: Harvard University Press, 1985). The major exception was feminists, who were far more radical in their ideology and leveling in their politics than any other group.

[16] Ibid., 189. Again, there is one exception: the media, who have a uniquely high opinion of their own powers of influence.

group expresses the true voice of the public; it follows also that one is somehow being kept from getting the message out. The circle of self-pity and self-adulation among groups of all sorts permeates American society. In politics, it validates public qualms about corruption and degeneration in the political realm, and leads to further cynicism about and withdrawal from political action, back to the realm of one's own personal "everybody" — that is, back to family and friends gathered together solely because they like one another. This attitude also fuels the characteristic American anxiety about conspiracies. If one's friends and colleagues are morally good and support America, then countergroups of evildoers must be working to undermine the nation, acting in hidden ways to keep "everybody" from power. This paranoia is exacerbated by the decentralization of the political system, which means that much of importance actually is undertaken out of the public eye, in informal meetings of the influential and powerful.

But although the pervasive paranoia of Americans about the perfidious nature of groups other than those they themselves belong to may be uncomfortable, it does not threaten the society at large with disruption. On the contrary, it makes it much harder for any group or representatives of a group to present themselves as saviors of the American way, and so provides a base for the mundane continuance of a social order based on trust of other Americans as individuals, along with distrust of them in groups or as leaders.[17] The voluntary and overlapping nature of group membership and the American emphasis on personal conscience and free choice also undercut the solidarity of any associations. Whatever the goals of the group, Americans believe deeply in the right of free entrance and free

[17] Tocqueville, *Democracy in America*, 194.

exit, and repudiate any association that denies members those rights.[18]

In general, then, despite the high ideals Americans hold about groups as the locus of caring and sharing, the culture is held together not by cohesive associations but by the infinite dispersal of weak and flexible personal links between individuals, who move freely between one group and another, searching for the elusive and often contradictory goals of loving community and personal self-satisfaction. These open group experiences give Americans practice at participating in community activism *when they want to* but permit detachment otherwise. The paranoia that often coincides with belonging may be unattractive, but it simply points out the real fragility of ties made primarily on the shaky grounds of affection. Sociologically speaking, such sentiments are far less harmful to the larger society than would be the case were strong commitments in place. Weak ties may not be heroic, but they also do not inspire fanaticism.

[18] Too little research has been done on changes in membership within groups. Wuthnow, *Sharing the Journey,* does describe how easily individuals can exit from self-help groups when the group moves beyond the provision of services to demanding serious commitments of time and effort.

Ethnicity as choice, race as destiny

Statistical Directive 15, issued in 1977, encourages Americans to classify themselves in the census as Native American, European, Afro-American, Asian, or Hispanic. Many have noted that this classification is arbitrary. It removes distinctions among Europeans, although that may by now have a measure of sense.[1] "Native" attribution must often be settled by court cases, since certain privileges now accrue to the category, though in the past the same identity was often repudiated. The situation for Hispanics is even more curious: as a purely linguistic grouping, it melds together the very different cultural backgrounds of Spain, Mexico, Puerto Rico, Cuba, and Latin America — including Portuguese-speaking Brazil. Asians are equally blended together in ways that do not conform to their own classifications. Meanwhile, Middle Easterners, Central Asians, South Asians, and other large groups of immigrants are left uncomfortably floating.

Identities are social constructions. The artificiality of these governmental categories does not necessarily mean that they will not lead to new self-images. In itself, this is not necessarily a bad thing: identities come and go, with many human beings possessing, consciously or not, multiple rather than singular identities. But great fear has resulted from the claim that these categories will become cages from which people will not be able to escape. As much of the mistrust of groups within American culture derives from the feeling that they contradict the central cultural premises of personal autonomy and voluntarism, the considerable hostility that has been directed to the politics of identity and difference is scarcely surprising. Casting

[1] S. Lieberson and M. Waters, *From Many Strands: Ethnic and Racial Groups in Contemporary America* (New York: Russell Sage Foundation, 1988); M. Waters, *Ethnic Options: Choosing Identities in America* (Berkeley: University of California Press, 1990); S. Lieberson and M. Waters, "The Ethnic Responses of Whites: What Causes Their Instability, Simplification, and Inconsistency?" *Social Forces* 72 (1993): 421–450.

light in this area matters greatly for our claim that most Americans share a culture: this would be nonsense if caged identities really are developing. Our response is simply that difference is *not* coming to characterize contemporary America. Despite official affirmations of pluralism, "America has a way of turning Greeks, Mexicans, Swedes, Chinese, and Polish Jews into reincarnations of seventeenth-century Englishmen."[2]

We can understand some of the reasons for this homogenizing process through a reconsideration of the way in which groups operate within American culture. The very fluidity of American society, Tocqueville noted, would press individuals toward immersion into artificial communities as a refuge from isolation. It is in this context that some Americans become concerned with their heritages, searching for meaning in what is considered to be the natural tie of blood kinship.[3] Yet, since the Second World War, intermarriage has become so common among European Americans that they are gradually being fused into a single "white" population. The statistics are striking: since 1950, 80 percent of Italian Americans, 75 percent of those with English, Irish, and Polish backgrounds, and 50 percent with a Jewish background marry outside their communities. This pattern allows individuals to decide which ancestors they wish to accentuate: for example, a person of Irish-Swedish-Portuguese-Serbian heritage might identify primarily as Irish, and fervently celebrate St Patrick's Day, wear the color green, read Irish literature, and enjoy Celtic music. This choice is then taken as derived from an innate affinity; the individual "feels" Irish and prefers to mingle with others with

---

[2] M. Lind, *The Next American Nation: The New Nationalism and the Fourth American Revolution* (New York: Free Press, 1995), 272.

[3] See D. Schneider, *American Kinship: A Cultural Account* (Chicago: University of Chicago Press, 1968), on the American cultural belief in the naturalness of blood ties.

the same heritage.[4] All this obviously has very little to do with Ireland and a great deal to do with the American quest for a meaningful sense of community. It is hard to recall amidst such mingling that these groups were considered different "races" a mere fifty years ago, and that signs reading "No Irish need apply" were a commonplace in urban settings.

In this atmosphere, it is not surprising that national tests of attitudes show that "responses from ethnic minorities are indistinguishable from those produced by the mainstream — except that minority respondents tend to be more traditional, more "American" in their value orientations."[5] This is not to say that distinctive "ethnic" practices have wholly disappeared in contemporary America. For example, Mexican Americans have much larger extended family units than average,[6] while Japanese Americans see themselves as being much more concerned with filial piety than their neighbors.[7] But even in these instances, the "traditional" practices are actually adaptions to the American context — they are not at all typical of the original homeland. "Ethnic" Americans characteristically construct dual identities, invoking imagined past practices in some con-

[4] Waters, *Ethnic Options.*

[5] H. Varenne, Introduction to H. Varenne, ed., *Symbolizing America* (Lincoln: University of Nebraska Press, 1986), x. For other recent anthropological arguments in favor of an American cultural identity, see J. Caughey, "Epilogue: On the Anthropology of America," in Varenne, *Symbolizing America,* J. L. Peacock, "American Cultural Values: Disorders and Challenges," in S. Forman, ed., *Diagnosing America: Anthropology and Public Engagement* (Ann Arbor: University of Michigan Press, 1994), and R. Rappaport, "Disorders of Our Own," in Forman, *Diagnosing America.*

[6] C. Velez-Ibanez, "Plural Strategies of Survival and Cultural Formation in U.S.-Mexican Households in a Region of Dynamic Transformation: The US-Mexico Borderlands," in Forman, *Diagnosing America.*

[7] S. Yanagisako, *Transforming the Past: Tradition and Kinship among Japanese Americans* (Stanford: Stanford University Press, 1985).

texts, and what they believe to be the practices of "ordinary Americans" in others.[8] Even though specific practices may symbolically set each group apart from all others, the pattern of self-manufacture is everywhere approximately the same. In each instance, idealized American values are partially adopted, while simultaneously the evocation of shared history and tradition serves as a way of differentiating the ethnic group from the mass society that surrounds it, providing a collective escape from the faceless marketplace by evoking imagined "essential" traditions.

In a real sense, then, although not strictly "voluntary," ethnic groups share much with the other associations so widespread in the United States. They, too, provide warmth, sharing, identity, and a modicum of belonging and affection to individuals coping with a mobile and competitive society. This background helps us to understand that the much-publicized development of multicultural education is very unlikely to Balkanize America.[9] The pedagogy of this movement, which has caused such unnecessary distress among conservative academics, emphasizes the subjective importance of ethnic identity by encouraging children to display their various heritages to one another for mutual approval—much in the way members of therapeutic groups reveal themselves in expectation of unconditional support. But the content of the "ethnicities" paraded in these displays is completely unthreatening to American ideals, and consists mainly of such innocuous items as food preferences, costumes, and holidays. Truly controversial

---

[8] Yanagisako, *Transforming the Past*; K. Blu, *The Lumbee Problem: The Making of an American Indian People* (Cambridge: Cambridge University Press, 1980).

[9] For a nonhysterical discussion of multicultural education, see N. Glazer, *We Are All Multiculturalists Now* (Cambridge: Harvard University Press, 1997).

items are resolutely kept off the agenda: Japanese children's books that feature murder and scatological jokes, for example, are forbidden. Multiculturalism is, in a nutshell, a consummately American phenomenon — one that celebrates and respects difference only so long as the differences are "nice" and not disruptive to smooth social interaction among equals.

It seems, then, that, despite all the publicity, for most white Americans, ethnicity remains a relatively weak identity marker, with very little content, although it has the very important subjective value of providing a vague personalized community in a world of diffuse and atomistic relationships. Although nominally an involuntary category, ethnicity in fact is chosen, at least among whites. Asians and other nonwhites have less choice, but for them, too, ethnicity is a haven supplied by manufactured "traditions" and shared tastes — not an encompassing cage, but a set of parameters that allows creative self-invention within the American framework. Like class and religion, ethnicity has minimal potential to develop into oppositional movements with any substantial alternative content. Rather, ethnic identity groups, like sexual identity organizations, religious sects, and twelve-step groups, are likely to multiply and subdivide, as hyphenated Americans select the communal identity that "feels best" to them. Ethnicity is different only in that it is liable to be seen as "really real" in the essentializing biological trope that Americans find so compelling.

If white ethnics can playfully choose their identities, and if Asian and Hispanic Americans can creatively explore the intersection between their own imagined "traditions" and an equally imagined America, the same is not the case for those who have negative identities thrust upon them.[10] This is the situation for African Americans, who are uniquely caged

[10] E. Goffman, *Stigma: Notes on the Management of Spoiled Identity* (Englewood Cliffs, N.J.: Prentice Hall, 1963).

within a devalued category. Although they have been in America from the very beginning, and have perhaps more claim than almost anyone else to be quintessentially American, African Americans still feel themselves to be excluded and discriminated against, despite legislation aimed at promoting their integration, and their own best efforts to participate. A few examples show that this feeling is not mistaken: in 1990 blacks constituted just over 12 percent of the population in the United States, yet held only 1.4 percent of political offices.[11] Prejudice is borne out in laboratory experiments wherein whites who see a videotape of a shove interpret it as violence from a black actor, play from a white one. Further experiments show that whites sit farther away from blacks, make speech errors in talking to them, have less eye contact, conduct shorter interviews, and evaluate their work as inferior.[12] Although fewer and fewer whites are willing to make overtly racist public statements, some recent estimates claim that up to a quarter of whites are still unrepentant bigots.[13] In the light of these facts, commentators have described America as a caste system that offers blacks no possibility of moving out of an

---

[11] A. Phillips, *The Politics of Presence* (Oxford: Oxford University Press, 1995), 87.

[12] J. Hochschild, *Facing Up to the American Dream: Race, Class, and the Soul of the Nation* (Princeton, N.J.: Princeton University Press, 1995), chap. 5.

[13] O. Patterson, *The Ordeal of Integration: Progress and Resentment in America's "Racial" Crisis* (Washington, D.C.: Counterpoint, 1997). See also D. Shipler, *A Country of Strangers: Blacks and Whites in America* (New York: Knopf, 1997), for a discussion of a 1990 University of Chicago study in which a cross-section of whites ranked racial and ethnic groups in order of intelligence, industriousness, and willingness to be self-supporting. Blacks were ranked lowest on all measures, with 53.2 percent of whites saying blacks were less intelligent than whites, 62.2 percent saying they were lazier, and 77.7 percent saying they were more willing to live on welfare.

imprisoning category, something that is a total repudiation of the central American values of equality and autonomy.[14]

This disturbing analysis gains even more credibility when we discover that those African Americans who have been integrated into middle-class society are more suspicious of whites than are poorer African Americans.[15] These individuals say that they are not accorded equal treatment by their white counterparts despite their financial success. This paradox has been discussed at length, but clearly a major reason is simply the fact that poor African Americans have very little real interaction with whites, and so can retain their illusions about their potential acceptance into white society; middle-class African Americans who have achieved relative economic success know that this has not occurred. Marriage patterns reveal a great deal. Intermarriage—the surest sign of assimilation—is rare between blacks and whites: in 1993 approximately 12 percent of all black marriages were to whites. In contrast, Asian Americans "marry out" more than 50 percent of the time.[16] It should be recalled in this context that anti-miscegeny laws, which were directed against marriage between whites and other races, were declared unconstitutional only in 1967, when fourteen states still had such laws on their books. All of these facts indicate that black Americans are right to believe themselves to be outsiders in their own country.

This is not to say, of course, that there have been no changes in the status of African Americans. Politically, even though

[14] J. Ogbu, *Minority Education and Caste: The American System in Cross-Cultural Perspective* (New York: Academic Press, 1978). The fact of cast-elike discrimination in America is evident in any number of ethnographic accounts, perhaps the best still being W. L. Warner et al., *Yankee City*, abridged ed. (New Haven: Yale University Press, 1963).

[15] Hochschild, *Facing Up to the American Dream*, chap. 4.

[16] S. Thernstrom and A. Thernstrom, *America in Black and White* (New York: Simon and Schuster, 1997), 523–27, 536.

blacks continue to be proportionally underrepresented, in absolute terms there has been a dramatic shift from the 500 African Americans elected to office in the early 1970s to over 6,800 elected in 1988.[17] Socially, relationships between whites and blacks are more humane than in the past. For example, in 1994, 73 percent of whites claimed they have a "good friend" who is black, compared with 9 percent in 1975.[18] Economically, African Americans have also had considerable recent success. In 1940 only 10 percent of black men could claim middle-class status; by 1960 the proportion had increased to 25 percent, and it now stands at 40 percent, with only 20 percent of black Americans below the poverty line.[19] Marriage to whites, though rare, has gone from 0.7 percent in 1963 to 12.1 percent in 1993; simultaneously, the number of whites who approve of such marriages has gone from 17 percent in 1968 to 45 percent in 1994.[20] But despite such positive signs, it is painfully evident that "the American dilemma" has not been solved. Predominantly black ghettos have become centers of catastrophe; half the murder victims and half those arrested for murder are black, though blacks comprise only 12 percent of the population; black poverty remains intractable, and black educational performance continues to lag behind that of whites.[21]

---

[17] Phillips, *Politics of Presence*, 87.

[18] Thernstrom and Thernstrom, *America in Black and White*, 521. In 1994, 78 percent of blacks had a good friend who was white, compared to 21 percent in 1975.

[19] Ibid., 81, 310.

[20] Ibid., 526, 524. The proportion of blacks approving cross-race marriage is 48 percent in 1968 and 68 percent in 1994.

[21] For a positive account of the African American situation in America, see ibid.; for a less sanguine discussion, see A. Hacker, *Two Nations: Black and White, Separate, Hostile, and Unequal* (New York: Scribner's, 1992). Patterson, *Ordeal of Integration*, is a particularly well-balanced account.

This unhappy situation is partly understandable as a bleak corollary of the blanket American faith in equality. To account for real inequality, or even for difference, Americans tend strongly to "naturalize" distinctions, making biology the source of differences that their ideology cannot otherwise explain.[22] We can see this tendency manifested in a benevolent form when white "hyphenated" ethnics claim innate biological characteristics for their chosen ethnic groups. Belonging then becomes "natural" and immutable, despite the real permeability and choice involved in ethnic categories. Obviously, once accepted, this categorizing technique can then be used to justify inequality and oppression. For example, anyone with one-sixteenth Japanese "blood" was automatically interred during the Second World War. Similarly, women can also be denigrated as naturally biologically inferior: "[I]f women are weak and emotional, it is *right* for men to control their bodies and wealth."[23] The premise of biological inferiority thus allows white male Americans to maintain their faith in human equality in the face of bigotry and oppression through the simple expedient of denying some people full human status.[24] This is

[22] See L. Dumont, *Homo Hierarchicus* (Chicago: University of Chicago Press, 1980), for a structural explanation based on his own experience of the hierarchical society of India. The biological argument has recently found new intellectual defenders in R. Hernstein and C. Murray, *The Bell Curve* (New York: Free Press, 1994). For a debate on this volatile issue, see S. Fraser, ed., *The Bell Curve Wars* (New York: Basic Books, 1995). Since Franz Boas, anthropologists have demonstrated that race as Americans understand it is above all a cultural construct, with no relation to biology. For recent statements on this, see the series of articles in the 1997–1998 editions of *American Anthropology Newsletter*.

[23] Hochschild, *Facing Up to the American Dream*, 34.

[24] See C. Lindholm, *The Islamic Middle East: An Historical Anthropology* (Oxford: Blackwell, 1996), for a discussion of the same mechanism in the Middle East.

most blatantly the case for African Americans, whose history of slavery, disproportionate poverty and high crime rate can be explained by an attributed essence. "Black blood," in this ideological construct, becomes an irredeemable stain, one that blemishes the whole character no matter in what small measure it exists — hence the "one-drop" rule, whereby anyone with a "black" ancestor is automatically reckoned to be black, regardless of appearance. According to this rule, it is perfectly possible for someone who is phenotypically white to "pass" for black; the reverse, however, is completely impossible. In other words, for Americans, anyone who looks black is black, but someone who looks white could also be black — if he or she has been polluted by "black blood."

The emphasis on essentializing blackness, as well as other racial classifications, is seen quite clearly in American census categories, which refuse to acknowledge mixed-race heritages, despite the fact that "30–70% of African-Americans by multi-generational history are multiracial; virtually all Latinos and Filipinos are multiracial, as are the majority of American Indians and Native Hawaiians."[25] The tendency toward essentializing has in some ways become more, rather than less, pronounced. For example, the 1870 census was divided into "white," "Chinese," "Indian," and "colored (blacks)," but it also provided a category for "colored (mulattos)." This distinction officially recognized the existence of an intermediate category of lighter-skinned free blacks. In urban areas, these "blue vein societies" — known also as the "four hundred" or "talented tenth" — had cultural dominance, intermarried among themselves, attended their own churches and colleges, and strove mightily to enter mainstream culture. But after 1920 the census dropped the "mulatto" category, and as a result "indi-

[25] M. Root, "Within, between, and beyond Race," in M. Root, ed., *Racially Mixed People in America* (Newbury Park, Calif.: Sage, 1992), 9.

viduals of more European phenotype gradually came to regard themselves, and were regarded, less as multiracial and more as light-skinned Blacks."[26] Members of these mixed-race groups still provide much of the leadership in the African American community, because of their educational and cultural credentials. The proud Frenchified Creoles of New Orleans and other areas of the Lower South followed a different trajectory, losing most of their very considerable wealth and prestige when they were legally merged with the larger black population. It is no accident that *Plessy v. Ferguson*, the case that upheld Jim Crow laws in 1896, involved Homer Plessy, a Louisiana Creole of one-eighth African American descent whose claims to equal treatment were repudiated by the Supreme Court.

But although the caging of African Americans within a negative racial category is a terrible blot on the American moral landscape, that does not mean that black Americans are not believers in American values. To the contrary, black opposition to cultural and economic oppression takes as its banner exactly the American premises that we have described: that people have a God-given right to manufacture their own identities and assert themselves within the social, economic, and political marketplace. Black Americans' belief that they can and should struggle against oppression and for justice and equity, articulated most powerfully by Martin Luther King, Jr., actually shows the extent of their acceptance of dominant values. Like other Americans, they believe in their personal right to pursue life, liberty, and happiness. African American "alienation has more in common with the spurned suitor," Jennifer Hochschild notes, "than with rejecting the object of desire."[27]

---

[26] G. R. Daniel, "Passers and Pluralists: Subverting the Racial Divide," in Root, *Racially Mixed People in America*, 97.

[27] Hochschild, *Facing Up to the American Dream*, 136.

Furthermore, while the premises of egalitarianism may press some whites toward categorizing blacks as inhuman, it has the reverse effect on others. That many white Americans can understand and sympathize with the plight of African Americans shows that racial prejudice or assertions of any form of innate inequality are never wholly legitimated within American culture. White support of policies designed to "level the playing field" has helped give blacks fair access to the mainstream. Yet it is equally clear that affirmative action, in particular, challenges other deeply held American values. We have already commented on the anti–special interest, anti-group attitude of Americans, who believe strongly in equality of individual opportunity, but strongly disapprove of privileges granted to any association — especially to one that makes its claims clamorously in public. African Americans are particularly subject to this form of disapproval: many whites, egged on by cynical politicians, increasingly believe that further benefits constitute an unfair advantage.[28] Prejudice is here added to a cultural trait, leading one to wonder whether much of the fuss made about multiculturalism serves as a mask for racism.

In response, some blacks have sought to find refuge in the very cage constructed for them by turning a negative identity into a positive one. Blackness, in this oppositional vision, becomes a genetic essence — a soul — that whites do not share. Radical Afrocentricists then claim that whites are diabolic, and that history itself is an insidious plot against the black race, who are the creators of all that is good and fine. Less radical claims are simply that there is an authentic, essential black identity, which must be maintained and nurtured. Thus Lani Guinier writes: "Authentic black leadership is . . . at its best, cultural[ly] similar to its constituency base. . . . [T]hey are po-

[28] J. Quadagno, *The Color of Welfare* (Oxford: Oxford University Press, 1994).

litically, psychologically and culturally black."[29] The danger here is that an emphasis on blackness as an authentic essence implicitly accepts the very fallacy of inescapable categories that authorized racism in the first place.[30] Nor does the argument for authenticity make it clear precisely what it means to be "politically, psychologically and culturally black" — especially when it is evident that even if African Americans "sometimes wish otherwise, all the world recognizes them as Americans."[31] Nonetheless, the affirmation of a separate black identity, coupled with continuing discrimination against blacks, remains the greatest challenge to America's core presumptions of egalitarian individualism.

Yet changes in the racial complexion of the American population may diffuse polarization and permit more class-based alliances. Increased intermarriage among blacks and whites, though remaining very low, has tripled between 1970 and 1990, increasing 30 percent during 1980–1990.[32] This may indicate that race is becoming less salient as an identity marker. More interestingly, in the most recent census, the racial category "Other" was the third fastest growing (a 45.1 percent increase since 1980), after the categories "Asian" and "Hispanic"; it was also the fourth largest in absolute numbers, after "white," "black," and "Hispanic."[33] Perhaps this means that

[29] L. Guinier, "The Triumph of Tokenism: The Voting Rights Act and the Theory of Black Electoral Success," *Michigan Law Review* 89 (1989): 1077, 1102–3, quoted in Lind, *Next American Nation*, 124.

[30] F. Fanon, *Black Skin, White Masks* (London: Macgibbon and Kee, 1968), remains the best and most poignant statement of the quandaries of racial identity.

[31] R. Gastril, "Cultural Regions of America," in L. S. Luedtke, ed., *Making America: The Society and Culture of the United States* (Chapel Hill: University of North Carolina Press, 1992), 141–42.

[32] Census 1991, table 54.

[33] Ibid., table 1.

more Americans wish to escape from racial categories altogether.[34] Another factor to take into account is the rapidly expanding Hispanic population. Research indicates that members of this group are generally far more willing to accept and sometimes even to esteem racial hybridity, thus erasing the black-white dichotomy. A transformation of racial categories may also result from the increased immigration into the United States of men and women from nonwhite regions, such as South Asia, Southeast Asia, the Caribbean, and Melanesia, as well as Africa. People from these areas, in common with many Hispanics, often have the dark skin pigmentation taken to be the "natural" mark of the African American, yet they will certainly make claims to have their own cultural and ethnic identities.[35] In short, heightened cultural and racial complexity will make it more and more difficult for either "blacks" or "whites" to assume that the world is easily divided into simple oppositional categories: Tiger Woods is certainly not the last

---

[34] Who exactly choose to designate themselves as "Other," remains unclear, but in C. Fernandez, "La Raza and the Melting Pot: A Comparative Look at Multiethnicity," (in M. Root, ed., *Racially Mixed People in America*) one census official is quoted as saying that "more than 96% of the 9.8 million people who declined to choose a particular race by checking the 'other race' box on the 1990 census forms were 'Hispanics'" (143). The following analysis owes much to Fernandez's work.

[35] This is occurring already in the United Kingdom, where divisions between "blacks" and "Asians" are complicating racial matters. See P. Werbner and T. Modood, eds., *Debating Cultural Hybridity: Multi-cultural Identities and the Politics of Anti-racism* (Atlantic Highlands, N.J.: Zed Books, 1997), for examples. M. Waters, "Ethnic and Racial Identities of Second-Generation Black Immigrants in New York City," *International Migration Review* 28 (1994): 795–820, finds a split amongst second-generation immigrants from the West Indies: some maintain an ethnic West Indian identity, while lack of opportunities drives others to identify themselves as African American.

Cablinasian. We can anticipate that in the long run the blurring of racial polarities will diffuse the layering of race, class, ghettoization, the historical scar of slavery, and the social inferiority that has so far kept anti-black prejudice powerful.

We note as well that white minority ethnic groups were themselves once seen as separate and inferior races. They were integrated into mainstream America in large measure because of their successful participation in the economy, which began when they provided unskilled labor in urban factories a hundred or more years ago. But before the Great Migration north, African Americans were segregated and immobilized on stagnant southern plantations. Although they have been in America for many generations, for historical reasons blacks have in a real sense only recently begun to follow the pathway already trodden by other minorities. For them, "late arrival into the wage labor category was in fact more significant for life chances than was late arrival into the society itself."[36]

If this is the case, the proper policy for America to follow to dispel racism is simple in principle: give black people every opportunity to find productive work.

This turns us finally to the vexing question of affirmative action, wherein the government actively intervenes to improve the lot of African Americans. As we have seen, such intervention has been attacked as privileging a group, thereby contradicting central American principles of individualism and equity.[37] The most nuanced defense of affirmative action has been mounted by Orlando Patterson, who argues that American faith in radical individualism obscures corporate respon-

---

[36] R. Williams, *Hierarchical Structures and Social Value: The Creation of Black and Irish Identities in the United States* (Cambridge: Cambridge University Press, 1990), 141.

[37] For data on this, see P. Sniderman and T. Piazza, *The Scar of Race* (Cambridge: Harvard University Press, 1993).

sibility, and that governmental intervention in natural disasters should logically permit governmental alleviation of historical disasters, such as slavery.[38] This is intellectually convincing, but it is likely to have little effect on majority opinion. Patterson realizes this, and moves toward what we, too, see as a more feasible approach, namely, that of appealing to precisely the values of fairness and individualism that are now being arrayed against affirmative action. This would mean giving no further help to middle-class blacks, but devoting every possible effort to aid those persons who are impoverished, prejudiced against, and marginalized—including people of *all* races.[39] We believe Americans can and will accept compensatory policies if they are universal.[40] This argument proposes gradually shifting the debate toward the destructive and inequitable consequences of poverty and prejudice per se and away from an emphasis on the reparation of racial discrimination—especially as race itself is becoming more and more indistinct as a category, though still retaining its unhappy capacity to mobilize divisive passions.

[38] O. Patterson, *The Ordeal of Integration: Progress and Resentment in America's 'Racial' Crisis* (Washington, D.C.: Counterpoint, 1997).

[39] It is worth stressing that the majority of poor Americans are not African American.

[40] For this argument, see George M. Fredrickson, "America's Caste System: Will It Change?" *New York Review of Books*, October 23, 1997, 68–75. As an example, while we were teaching at Harvard, an award was offered to African American students. The award was given on the basis of grade point average, which was considered to be an objective criterion for excellence. As a result, the recipients were inevitably upper-class individuals who had benefited from superb preparatory schools. Similarly, Harvard has an enviable record of African American enrollment percentage-wise, but those who enroll are, on the average, wealthier and better educated than their white counterparts. Of course, this is a travesty of affirmative action, but it makes the point that a more class-based awards system would be both fairer and more inclusive.

Two cheers for homogeneity

Some reflections on the notion of civil society allow us to underscore our argument. Discussion can take off from a characteristically brilliant argument by Daniel Bell asserting that the United States is *nothing but* a civil society.[1]

There is a good deal of sense to this: the diffusion of conflict within society results, as noted in Part One, in a plurality of groups whose interests are not united against an overbearing state. But we have stressed quite as much something missed by Bell, namely, the presence of a cultural frame that privileges accommodation rather than conflict. We argue that wide acceptance of that frame plays as significant a part in limiting conflict as does the sheer fact of pluralism. But a more subtle point follows from a fuller definition of civil society.[2] Civil society is not, as the traditional definition has it, the mere presence of strong and autonomous groups within society. Instead, it depends upon a particular social consensus to agree to live together despite genuine difference. The greatest example of such an agreement in European history remains the Treaty of Westphalia in 1648: after the realization that neither side could win the religious wars, religion was relegated to the private realm, thereby accommodating divergent views.[3]

From this perspective, we can see that the United States is not a civil society in the fullest sense, though it is indeed a society where — except for the obscene exception of racism — very great personal civility is practiced. In spite of the plethora of noisy interest groups, there is little actual recognition,

[1] D. Bell, "'American Exceptionalism' Revisited: The Role of Civil Society," *Public Interest* 95 (1989): 38–56.

[2] For this definition, see J. A. Hall, "In Search of Civil Society," in J. A. Hall, ed., *Civil Society: Theory, History, Comparison* (Oxford: Polity Press, 1995).

[3] E. Gellner, *Civil Society and Its Rivals* (London: Hamish Hamilton, 1994), chap. 5.

whether resigned or enthusiastic, of genuinely alternative ways of life. This point can be underscored by recalling a standard European joke about American foreign policy: the United States wishes people to be free to choose, just so long as they choose the American way! This is scarcely surprising: the American experience has not been that of the clash of utterly different ways of life, except for the challenges from the South and from the working class, both of which were so completely destroyed. Such differences as do exist in America, though passionately embraced, are objectively relatively small: while ideologically "all are different," Americans in fact are remarkably "all the same." The homogenizing powers of this framework have been astonishing, as can be highlighted by recalling John Kennedy's amazing claim that his Catholicism presented no obstacles to his political career: this is a typically American "Protestant" assertion that religion is a matter of private conscience. More generally, it is worth noting that the greatest problem facing most believers (including members of the Jewish faith) is not persecution, but maintaining any identity whatsoever. Homogenization by the extension of the American values of individual choice may soon apply even to sexual preference, which may become yet another life style option for Americans, thus eroding the remains of the solidarity of the gay community.[4]

It seems then that an emphasis on excessive individualism as a description of America is quite far from the mark.[5] But atten-

---

[4] The recent effort to biologize homosexuality renders gay identity innate, and thus works to prevent exit.

[5] In many senses, David Riesman's famous characterization of Americans as other-directed is line with our argument, though he did not stress the deep cultural values that underlie American conformity as much as we do, and saw a more radical discontinuity between past and present than

tion should also be paid to those who demand prescriptively a diminution of commonality within American culture.[6] Uncritical praise for a "politics of difference" is hopelessly naive, wrongly presuming lower-level group identities to be naturally pleasant and imagining that contacts among such groups will remain civilized without the presence of any rules of the game. We are not of this party, and believe instead that no harsh judgment should be made about the powerful homogenizing and accommodative forces at work within American culture. For one thing, it is well to remember that the seventeenth-century European invention of the ideal of toleration was followed first by the ideological surge of the French revolutionary period, and then by fascism and communism, the two great totalitarian movements of the twentieth century.[7] In contrast, America's homogenizing capacities have ensured that its internal conflicts have *not* led either to world war or to tyranny. Accordingly, there is much to be said for the decencies of a little dullness and the comforts of a measure of conformity. For

---

we have seen (see the 1961 edition of D. Riesman, with N. Glazer and R. Denney, *The Lonely Crowd* [New Haven: Yale University Press]). Riesman's argument that a change had taken place from an inner-directed to an other-directed character type is best understood, in our view, as an ecologically motivated shift within the same character type. Frontier populations (and other populations under pressure and at risk) express egalitarian individualism as self-affirmation; settled and prosperous communities practice instead moral minimalism and seek to avoid conflict. Both modes are homogenizing and conformist, though the latter certainly becomes more prevalent in circumstances of stability and affluence.

[6] J. Tully, *Strange Multiplicity* (Cambridge: Cambridge University Press, 1995).

[7] It should also be noted that the return to civil society in Europe has owed a very great deal to a geopolitical settlement that depended and still depends upon the United States.

another, American homogenization has been to a universal ideal, which has diminished ethnic particularism. If only this incredible capacity for absorbing difference could be extended to allow African Americans full entry into American life! That this has not yet happened explains why we offer only two cheers for homogeneity.

Conclusion

The main burden of our argument is clear: America is not in any danger of breaking apart. Historical processes have worked to solidify and stabilize powerful central institutions, while suppressing possible sources of resistance. Class loyalties, so important in European politics, have been eclipsed in America, where the vast majority lump themselves together as "middle class" and assume themselves to be in general agreement on fundamental principles.[1] The central challenge to industrial capitalism was defeated at the end of the nineteenth century. In the postwar years, the scandal of de jure segregation was ended, but this has not been followed by the creation of any lasting alliance amongst the less advantaged as whole. Despite the rhetorical flourishes of academic multiculturalists, potentially disruptive ethnic, religious, and racial differences have been offset by the great, vague promise of the American creed and by the relative absence of any concentrated groups of angry and humiliated minorities, although the experience of African Americans stands as a partial exception to this rule. In general, America has succeeded in diffusing the overlapping sources of difference and discontent that have played such a compelling and harmful role in Europe. It is no surprise that "[m]ost Americans remain highly patriotic and religious, believe they are living in the best society in the world, and think that their country and economy, in spite of problems, still offer them opportunity and economic security."[2]

This does not mean that all is sweetness and light. The United States, like every other living society, is torn by the

---

[1] On middle-class values, see A. Wolfe, *One Nation, After All* (New York: Viking, 1998); C. Perin, *Belonging in America: Reading between the Lines* (Madison: University of Wisconsin Press, 1988); D. McCloskey, "Bourgeois Virtue," *American Scholar* (Spring 1994): 177–91.

[2] S. M. Lipset, *American Exceptionalism: A Double-Edged Sword* (New York: Norton, 1996), 287–88. Wolfe, *One Nation, After All*, offers more recent evidence of the general satisfaction of Americans with their society.

contradictory implications of its fundamental values: the denunciation of politicians and suspicion of the political realm corresponds with the high expectations Americans have of politics; the periodic witch hunts and upsurges of enthusiasm are mirror images of political apathy; an emphasis on personal ties is accompanied by paranoia about groups other than one's own. Most painfully, a tendency to essentialize differences and to indulge in racism paradoxically coincides with egalitarian ideals; meanwhile, attempts to affirm a recompensatory politics of group recognition clash with deep values of individualism and equity. Other, related tensions could be cited: the recourse to crime as a route of social mobility reflects urgent desires for competitive success; the American romance with rebellion and risk is expressed in young people's emulation of the styles of ghetto gangs; drug and alcohol use is a perpetual temptation for individualists seeking personal salvation; the rise of self-help groups and therapeutic fads is a modern manifestation of an old American quest for frontiers to conquer, and so on.

Such quandaries characterize American society. They provoke anxiety, disrupt life, and require remedial action; but they are not — with the possible exception of African American alienation — threats to the social fabric as such. They are only felt to be so because Americans discount the nation's stability and do not realize the homogenizing power of their own culture. One of our students once remarked proudly, "We Americans do not have a culture; we are all different," blithely unaware of the fact that no statement could be more American. This blindness derives from assumptions that all persons are equally distinctive, unique and endowed with freedom to pursue their individual quests for happiness and redemption. From these premises, community is understood to be built up by the voluntary cooperation of individual actors. This model of community naturally discounts that which is shared and makes

Americans anxious about cohesion. The present discourse of collapse is an expression of this characteristic uneasiness.

If warnings of disintegration are useless as analyses, they do tell us something about an aspect of the American experience.[3] Most obviously, the rhetoric of breakdown has inherited its moralistic tone from the first American intellectuals: Calvinist preachers. Modern critics, whether on the left or the right, tend to sound like Jeremiahs, self-righteously calling on Americans to rise above their sinful natures.[4] More generally, behind the discourse of disintegration lie elitist fears of democracy as practiced by real people. Intellectuals can often feel themselves twice marginalized in America, by capitalism and by egalitarianism, and imagine alternate worlds where they, rather than the fat cats and vulgar yahoos, would be recognized as leaders and exemplars. Of late, this tendency has been heightened by rampant American economic and political success, which further peripheralizes academics who are not economists or political scientists. And of course, affluence also awakens deep-seated Calvinistic fears of backsliding and corruption. Thus we have the paradox of rising disquiet during a period when American might is clearly in the ascent.

Our approach has been akin to that of a rather more hopeful and less evangelical school of historians and social scientists, included in whose number are Richard Hofstader, Louis Hartz, Daniel Bell, and Seymour Martin Lipset. In their various works, they have emphasized American exceptionalism, stressing the American middle-class consensus in favor of individualism, equality, and liberty. While they have worried about

[3] R. Wilkinson, *The Pursuit of American Character* (New York: Harper and Row, 1988).

[4] S. Bercovitch, *The American Jeremiad* (Madison: University of Wisconsin Press, 1978).

American tendencies toward a paranoid and anti-intellectual style of popular politics, present in McCarthyism and in anti-Semitism more generally,[5] these authors have usually insisted that the pursuit of wealth and the diversity of society undermine the politics of resentment.

Although we share something with this view, our characterization of American life is less rosy. We prefer to state firmly that American life combines political equality with a structure of social inequality. Nor do we believe that the consensus of American life was predetermined at the start: rather, genuine societal alternatives were defeated by violent means. Furthermore, the idea that demagogic popular forces represent danger is vastly overdone, for all that a moralizing strain in American life has led to bitter conflicts, as witnessed in violent confrontations over abortion, gun control, and race. But these feuds have been over interpretations of the American creed, not over its existence. They test the framework, and are salutary in pressing the public to consider the actual implications of their vague beliefs. We believe that Americans have less to fear from the messiness and occasional violence of popular protests and movements than they do from the machinations of anti-democratic elites. There was, for example, nothing paranoid or unreasonable in the ideas of collective rights that workers fought for at the end of the nineteenth century, and those who defeated them represented less civilization than the interests of big capital. It is equally clear that segregation would still exist if not for the moral fervor of the civil rights movement. To argue in this tone is not to embrace any easy populism: popular forces can be vicious. But so, too, can political elites. McCarthyism owed less to popular passion and more to the support of wealthy right-wing businesspeople, who bankrolled his

---

[5] A quite understandable fear, given the Jewish heritage of almost all of these writers.

anti-Communist witch hunt.[6] When the general public was actually able to witness McCarthy's posturing on television, it was quick to disown him. Nor should foreign policy be left in the hands of experts. Popular voices have occasionally been both intemperate and ignorant in this arena, but any realistic assessment of foreign policy in the postwar years ought to recognize that the key mistakes were made by an autonomous political elite, with mass protests deserving praise for rescuing America from its debacle in Southeast Asia.

Our own conclusion is that the greatest problem of American culture is its inability to conceptualize and deal with inequality. This is the best place to make a crucial point about the way in which the two parts of this book fit together. Bluntly, American culture serves as a perfect mask for the structure of interests, permitting considerable harshness and injustice because of its ideology of egalitarian individualism. Even though resentment can be shown to the rich, little is done to disempower them because wealth is seen to result from character rather than from class advantage, and because ordinary Americans participate in the democratization of consumption. Added to this has been the centrality of racism within American culture. If the biologizing of difference has passed its peak, it has been replaced by a value system that scorns the "undeserving" poor and makes it all too easy to continue to stigmatize African Americans.

Not surprisingly, we would prefer a society that is less racist and more egalitarian. However, we are well aware that the bulk of our argument suggests that any unified action of the poor to redistribute income is less than likely, in part because racial prejudice is still deeply embedded in the national fabric. This is discouraging. Yet it is equally true that Americans con-

---

[6] M. P. Rogin, *The Intellectuals and McCarthy* (Cambridge: MIT Press, 1967).

tinue to believe in and to act upon their sacred principles of equality, freedom, and justice. This enduring tension between reality and ideal may yet fuel progressive social change.

Dreams are easy, but their realization is difficult. Our task here has been to prepare the ground by drawing a clear picture, as free from moralizing as possible, of the structure and culture of the United States, seen in historical perspective. We have done so in the belief that without first understanding how a society functions, it is impossible to change it for the better.

Index

abolitionists: attempt to impeach Johnson, 40; charges of northern, 33; popularity of idea of abolition, 38–39, 75

affirmative action: as challenge to American values, 140; government intervention under, 143; Patterson's defense of, 143–44

African Americans: change in status of, 135–36; excluded by culture, 82; impact of war on, 64; integrated into middle-class society, 135; during Johnson administration, 65–66; lack of separatist claims by, 45; moving out of urban ghettos, 69; negative identity thrust upon, 133–35; recent economic success, 136. *See also* blacks

Agnew, Spiro, 68

Alien and Sedition Act (1798), 28, 52

American creed: Americans' assumptions about, 84; beliefs of, 93–94; conflict over interpretations of, 152

American Federation of Labor (AFL), 56–57

Americanism as a religion, 91–92

anti-Communism, 71

anti-miscegenist laws, 135

anti-Semitism, 152

anti-slavery sentiment, 33

Asians: native attribution, 129

associations, voluntary: American ambivalence toward, 123; condominium, 124; effect of proliferation of (Tocqueville), 123; events within, 125; for single-issue politics, 116; Tocqueville's perception of, 123–24

autonomy, 102

Bell, Daniel, 145, 151

Bellah, Robert, 4

Bercovitch, Secvan, 93

blacks: excluded from New Deal policy, 42; Great Migration from the South, 43, 63; post-Civil War voting, 40; riots of whites against, 64; in Union forces, 39. *See also* African Americans

Boorstin, Daniel, 88

Bryan, William Jennings, 54–55

capitalism: authority of American, 36; challenge to industrial, 47; corporate mergers, 50; Gompers's view of, 56–57; role of New Deal in saving American, 58

capitalist class: smashing of labor strikes by, 55–56

census categories, American, 138–39

Chesterton, G. K., 91

Chinese Exclusion Act (1882), 57

Civil Rights Act (1875), 41

civil rights movement: effect of, 76; in the South, 64–65

civil society: absence in Soviet Union, 77–78; America as, 145; dependent on social agreement, 145

Civil War: issues precipitating, 37–39; outcome of, 31, 41–42, 75

class: anti-aristocratic legislation and sentiment, 22–23; existence in colonial America, 17–18. *See also* working class

Clayton Act (1914), 57

Clinton, Bill, 88

Cohen, Leonard, 9

DATE DUE

GAYLORD

PRINTED IN U.S.A.